Looking Closely

Looking Closely

Exploring the Role of Phonics in One Whole Language Classroom

Heidi Mills
University of South Carolina

Timothy O'Keefe
Columbia, South Carolina, Public Schools

Diane Stephens
University of Illinois at Urbana-Champaign

National Council of Teachers of English
1111 Kenyon Road, Urbana, Illinois 61801

For Sandra Pees and David Whitin, dear friends and two of our most influential teachers.

NCTE Editorial Board: Richard Abrahamson, Celia Genishi, Joyce Kinkead, Louise Wetherbee Phelps, Gladys V. Veidemanis, Charles Suhor, *ex officio*, Michael Spooner, *ex officio*

Manuscript Editor: Jane M. Curran

Production Editor: Rona S. Smith

Book Design: Doug Burnett

NCTE Stock Number 30313-3050

It is the policy of NCTE in its journals and other publications to provide a forum for the open discussion of ideas concerning the content and the teaching of English and the language arts. Publicity accorded to any particular point of view does not imply endorsement by the Executive Committee, the Board of Directors, or the membership at large, except in announcements of policy, where such endorsement is clearly specified.

The work upon which this publication was based was supported in part by the Office of Educational Research and Improvement under Cooperative Agreement No. G0087-C1001-90 with the Reading Research and Education Center and the Center for the Expansion of Language and Thought. The publication does not necessarily reflect the views of the agencies supporting the research.

Library of Congress Cataloging-in-Publication Data
Mills, Heidi.
     Looking closely : exploring the role of phonics in one whole language classroom / Heidi Mills, Timothy O'Keefe, Diane Stephens.
        p.   cm.
     Includes bibliographical references (p.).
     1. Reading (Elementary)—Phonetic method—Case studies.
2. Language experience approach in education—Case studies.
3. Language arts (Elementary)—Case studies. I. O'Keefe,
Timothy. II. Stephens. Diane. III. Title.
LB1573.3.M55 1992
372.4'145—dc20   91-42385
                                                    CIP

Contents

Foreword by Jerome C. Harste   vii

Preface   xi

Acknowledgments   xvii

1. Introduction by Timothy O'Keefe   1

2. Highlighting the Role of Graphophonemics
   on a Typical Day   4

3. Tracing the Language Growth of Three Children   26

4. Teaching in Support of Learning   52

Afterword   65

References   67

Authors   69

Foreword

Whole language teachers have been more successful in empowering children than in changing power relations in the profession. Similarly, whole language teachers have always been more successful in raising political awareness than in changing the politics of literacy. This book is yet another attempt on the part of whole language people to dress for success. It is a testimonial to the fact that the world of reading is changing.

I love theory. I love kids. Good teachers and good books simply take my breath away.

Heidi Mills, Tim O'Keefe, and Diane Stephens are, I am proud to say, my students. They all studied at Indiana University. Heidi Mills and Tim O'Keefe met in my undergraduate reading and language arts class. Later they got married and have lived happily ever after.

After setting up and teaching in a highly successful whole language early childhood program in Michigan, Heidi Mills returned to Indiana University to get her doctorate. She is now teaching and researching at the University of South Carolina in Columbia.

Tim O'Keefe has had a successful teaching career in three states. Experienced in grades K–6, he has taught effectively in compensatory, transition, and Head Start programs. Tim is a tremendous teacher, as this book so vividly shows. He is a featured teacher in several of the videotapes that I have produced at Indiana University.

Diane Stephens, who had taught reading in a variety of settings, both public and private, came to Indiana University from New York to study semiotics. After receiving her Ph.D., she taught at the University of North Carolina–Wilmington, where she developed an interdisciplinary clinic. She is now teaching and researching at the Center for the Study of Reading at the University of Illinois at Urbana-Champaign.

Together these authors are a living testimonial to the fact that whole language is both changing and spreading. They and their book are proof that sometimes it takes a new generation to make real change.

Mills, O'Keefe, and Stephens do for whole language what neither I nor my generation of whole language advocates could do:

they present a sane and practical discussion of the role of phonics in good whole language classrooms. Good teachers everywhere will find it invaluable.

Looking Closely: Exploring the Role of Phonics in One Whole Language Classroom addresses two important issues: (1) the role that phonics plays in reading and in learning to read and (2) how phonics is handled in whole language classrooms.

Phonics and Learning to Read

The content of this book is rooted in the language stories and literacy lessons of our observations of children learning to read. At age three, for example, my daughter could spot a McDonald's from a distance of one mile. In fact, her ability to spot a McDonald's made us plan our outings quite carefully.

From the time that he could talk, my son asked me to read the insignia on every car we passed. I noticed that he was reading at age three when one day he said "Chevrolet" as we came up to a car at a stoplight. Despite this success, right before entering second grade he needed tutorial help to be able to do the phonics worksheets that were required in his school.

I visited a kindergarten classroom the other day. A group of about eight children was discussing three books that teachers had read them about the moon. Phonics people would say that they could not *really* read because they could not sound out each of the words in the books themselves. Despite this, they certainly could discuss the books and they certainly had opinions about the books which they did not mind sharing. I caught myself wondering why some people would not want to call these kids *readers*. They definitely had access to the reading process. What a shame it would be to tell them that they were not readers because they did not control the graphophonemic system of language.

These and other issues are at the heart of different approaches to reading instruction. As Mills, O'Keefe, and Stephens show, the issue is not really phonics versus no phonics, but whether or not explicit instruction in sound-symbol relationships should be the primary focus of our reading programs.

Phonics and the Whole Language Classroom

In my judgment, whole language has always accommodated phonics, but phonics has never accommodated whole language. Given my feelings, it is not surprising that my first reaction to this book was, "Fine—but where is the book that shows how teachers who use a phonics approach deal with the insights into reading and learning to read underlying whole language? Where, for example, is the book that assures us that teachers who teach reading through a phonetic approach are making sure that children see reading as functional and meaningful? Where is the book that shows how phonics advocates are making sure that they are connecting kids with books for life? Where is the book that shows how phonics advocates have stopped silencing children through recognition that there are other cue systems in language that children already master and that they can build from this base? Where is the book that shows teachers how to counteract the negative ripple effect that phonics instruction has on reading comprehension?"

As I read further, I realized that this book was not an attempt to end or even to enter into the phonics/whole language debate. Rather, it is a simple, clear, and elegant statement of what the profession has come to know about how children learn about the graphophonemic system of language and what role such knowledge plays in the reading process.

Looking Closely: Exploring the Role of Phonics in One Whole Language Classroom is meant to reassure those teachers who think whole language ignores phonics as well as to provide examples of how one whole language teacher helps children in his classroom learn about the graphophonemic system of language within the context of real reading, writing, and learning engagements.

And it does this very well. I hope that this book is read widely—by teachers new to whole language as well as those steeped in it; by undergraduate students first learning about whole language as well as returning veterans; by preservice as well as inservice teachers; by advocates as well as skeptics of whole language.

The authors of this text take seriously the whole language tenet that "no one becomes literate without personal involvement in literacy." They remind teachers that phonics is a natural part of both language learning and language teaching. They invite readers to make connections, to rethink instruction, to grow.

The function of a foreword, like the function of this book, is to give perspective. I hope that I have done for this book what Mills, O'Keefe, and Stephens do for whole language. But you be the judge. In the meantime, I am ordering copies. Mills, O'Keefe, and Stephens may be right. There may well be no limits to the kinds of success one can dress for. It is, after all, a new generation.

Jerome C. Harste
Indiana University

Preface

When people meet and talk about reading and writing, the terms *phonics* and *whole language* often come up in the discussion. Whether the two are compatible or incompatible depends on the meanings individuals have for those terms. Sometimes people talk about phonics as if it means "decontextualized direct instruction which focuses on the set of rules establishing the relationship between sounds of letters and their names." When phonics carries this meaning, phonics and whole language are not compatible. However, most of the time the word *phonics* is used to mean "knowledge about sound-symbol relationships in language." When phonics is defined this way, phonics and whole language are quite compatible. Indeed, in the models that Jerome C. Harste and Carolyn L. Burke (1977, 38) developed to explain cue systems in language (see Figure 1), they showed how knowledge about sound-symbol relationships is one of the three cue systems, one of the three interrelated means, which readers use to make meaning from print. The other two cue systems are syntax and semantics.

Harste and Burke explained that when language is kept whole (rather than divided into often meaningless small parts), readers use all three cue systems together. Consider the sentence "Mary and Tom took a long walk down the tree-lined _____." Using their knowledge of the syntax, or grammar of language, readers can predict what might come next in the sentence. Indeed, it is not necessary for readers to know or even to have heard the words *syntax* or *syntactic* or *grammar* to be able to figure out that the last word will be some sort of thing. This knowledge about language is what Harste and Burke referred to as the syntactic cue system.

Knowledge of the world provides semantic cues. By focusing on what the sentence means, readers can predict what noun might fit in the sentence. Mary and Tom could be walking down a tree-lined street—or path, or road, or sidewalk. Readers consistently make these kinds of predictions.

Graphophonemic knowledge, or knowledge of sound-symbol relationships, allows readers to verify their predictions. The very first letter of the word narrows the range of possibilities. Seeing the *p* of *path* eliminates *street, road,* and *sidewalk.* Should the

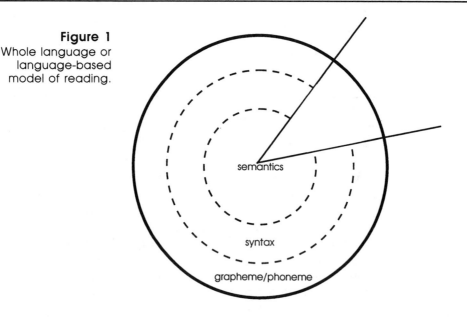

Figure 1
Whole language or
language-based
model of reading.

semantics

syntax

grapheme/phoneme

reader encounter a *b* (as in *boulevard*), new hypotheses will be made.

Language Learning

In all authentic reading and writing events, language is kept whole and all cue systems are accessed. This parallels language learning outside of reading instruction. Indeed, Michael Halliday (1982) argues that in those naturally occurring situations, when language is being used to serve some function for the user, speakers and listeners, readers and writers simultaneously learn language, learn about language, and learn through language.

Once people understand that phonics, when defined as knowledge about sound-symbol relationships, is a critical part of learning language, questions then arise about how whole language teachers help children learn about language. In particular, people want to know how whole language teachers help children learn about sound-symbol relationships.

The first answer is that whole language teachers are very knowledgeable about language and learners and learning. Indeed, many whole language teachers have taken course work in such fields as psycholinguistics, sociolinguistics, cognitive and developmental psychology, learning theory, and semiotics. Using this knowledge base, whole language teachers set up their classrooms so that children have ample opportunities to engage with texts and to learn through that engagement. In this way, children learn about reading by reading and about writing by writing; and in the process of each, they also learn about the other. Frank Smith (1978) calls this "reading like a writer" and "writing like a reader."

The second answer is that these informed whole language teachers are also careful "kidwatchers" (Y. Goodman 1985) and use their knowledge base to reflect on their observations of children and to make informed instructional decisions. They might ask themselves, for example, what a particular child seems to know about language already, or what hypothesis the child seems to be currently testing.

The third answer is that whole language teachers are artful at moving their understanding of language, learning, and learners into practice. They might follow their kidwatching with questions about how best to help that child, about whether to intervene or stay in the background, about what kinds of new experiences and demonstrations would be helpful.

None of these answers, however, addresses what many teachers are asking. What they want to know is what learning and teaching about phonics *looks like* in a whole language classroom. Just what is it, they ask, that whole language teachers *do*? What do the children *do*?

It would be wonderful if these teachers could sit in whole language classrooms and see firsthand how whole language teachers help children learn about sound-symbol relationships in language. However, in many communities, there are not yet whole language classrooms in which to observe. In still others, teachers are not given the release time that would make it possible for them to leave their classrooms and visit the classrooms of others.

Texts and/or videotapes could meet that need. However, at the time this book was conceived, there were no books or videos that specifically addressed the questions that teachers had about phonics in whole language classrooms. We therefore decided to write a book that would allow teachers to "visit" one whole language classroom and see how one teacher helped children learn about sound-symbol relationships in language.

We chose to use the word *phonics* in the title of our book because that was the word most teachers used to ask about what we referred to as "sound-symbol" or "graphophonemic" relationships. Throughout the book, we more often use the latter terms since those words tie to our knowledge base about language and to our understanding of written language as having three cue systems.

Overview of the Book

Tim O'Keefe begins the book with an introduction to his classroom and his philosophy. In the chapters that follow, we examine his classroom from three perspectives: In chapter 2, we describe a typical day, April 19, 1990, so that readers can have a sense of how children learn about letter-sound relationships across the day. We also examine the various curricular elements that support this learning. Next, in chapter 3, we look at the growth of three children over the course of a year, providing readers with an opportunity to understand how the learning of many days gets played out in the lives of individual children. Last, in chapter 4, we make explicit the role of the teacher, so that teaching and learning about grapheme-phoneme relationships from a whole language perspective might be more easily understood.

We chose to focus on Tim's whole language classroom for several reasons. First, he extensively documents and reflects upon what happens in his classroom. His records, combined with his field notes and videotapes taken by coauthor Heidi Mills and David Whitin, her colleague at the University of South Carolina, enable us to draw an accurate portrait of the complexities of Tim's curriculum. Second, since most of the questions about the role of phonics in whole language classrooms are focused on young children, we thought it would be helpful to provide readers with a close look at six year olds. Third, the children in Tim's classroom had all been identified as "at-risk." While there have been some suggestions that these "different" children need fundamentally "different" instruction (see, for example, Stahl, Osborn, and Lehr 1990), Tim's data, in contrast, suggest that the learning of his "at-risk" students parallels what we know about nonlabeled children. Fourth, we wanted authentic examples of instruction from an actual classroom. Tim, Heidi, and David were initially united by an interest in whole language and so began by focusing on a supportive reading and writing curriculum. They soon realized that they could apply to mathematics much of what they were learning about language and language instruction. Since then they have been developing a mathematics curriculum that is theoretically consistent with whole language (see Whitin, Mills, and O'Keefe 1990). What this means is that while the data shared here were not specifically collected to document teaching and learning about phonics, we (coauthors Heidi, Tim, and Diane) were able to use the data for that purpose because teaching and learning about sound-symbol relationships was as authentically embedded in the data as it was in Tim's curriculum.

All this seems fairly straightforward except for this: In order to write collaboratively, we all had to use the third person when referring to Heidi (which did not happen often) and to Tim (which happened *very* often). (Diane had simply instigated the collaboration, was not part of the classroom itself, and so did not get talked about at all.) While the use of the third person made many things easier and less cumbersome, it also had the unfortunate effect of homogenizing our voices. In particular, Tim's voice, which Heidi and Diane felt strongly should be emphasized, seemed muted when Tim was always *he* and never *I.*

After considering several different solutions, all of which felt contrived and made the writing uneven, we decided to keep the third person throughout the jointly authored chapters. By doing so, as well as by sharing with the reader our decisions about voice, we hope to highlight the fact that the text was collaboratively rather than cooperatively written, while acknowledging the central role that Tim played both as teacher and as author. Tim's solo voice is heard in chapter 1.

Our goals for this collaboratively written text are, however, straightforward. We are concerned that a large number of people—teachers, children, administrators, parents, legislators—want to understand the relationship between graphophonemic information and whole language. Our text shows how one teacher helps children learn about sound-symbol relationships in language. And while each example highlights that particular cue system in language, each example also reveals how all the cue systems in language are present in all whole language events.

For example, Tony's letter to his pen pal, discussed further in chapter 2 (see Figure 5 on page 20), demonstrates Tony's knowledge about syntax, about semantics, and about graphophonemic relationships. In his letter, Tony uses several types of sentence structures, all of which reveal his understanding of English syntax ("It looks like you got a ring"; "Can you send me another letter on the computer?" "I can't wait for the pen pal party"; "Love, Tony"). In addition, his sentences are all meaningful—they convey the various messages that Tony wishes to communicate to his pen pal. Tony's use of the semantic cue system is also revealed in his reading of his letter. He begins, reads the first five sentences and part of the sixth ("It will be ever . . ."), notices that what he has read does not make sense, looks carefully at his text, realizes he has skipped a line, and rereads ("[You] will be my very best pen pal I ever met, pen pal"). Tony's letter also reveals his extensive knowledge of grapheme-phoneme relationships. In the forty-eight-word text, the spelling of thirty-three words is completely conventional. The other fifteen words provide a window into what Tony knows about spelling conventions and what he is exploring through invented spelling. Most of those words are spelled as they sound: *s-i-n-d* for *send; s-u-m* for *some; w-a-t* for *wait; l-l-e-k* for *like; c-o-m* for *come.*

Our text, however, is not an introduction to linguistics (although teachers interested in supporting children as language users might want to take such a course), nor does it detail or reveal all that the children in Tim's classroom learn about language. It is simply a close look at how one teacher helps children learn about sound-symbol relationships in his whole language classroom.

We hope that this visit with Tim contributes to the reader's understanding of the relationship between the graphophonemic cue system and whole language.

Heidi Mills
Timothy O'Keefe
Diane Stephens

Acknowledgments

Given that knowledge is socially constructed, multiple voices and perspectives influenced the creation of this text. Although our voices are in the foreground, we would like to acknowledge others who have touched this piece.

We would like to begin by thanking the teachers who persisted in asking questions about the role of phonics in whole language. They pushed us to consider issues in whole language from their perspective and challenged us to revisit fundamental aspects of our model.

We are also appreciative for the feedback we received on our initial drafts. Connie Weaver, Carolyn Burke, Jerry Harste, Beverly Busching, Yetta Goodman, Colleen Gilrane, Phyllis Wilkin, Jean Osborne, and Judith Newman all contributed to important conversations that led to several revisions. Since they all generated unique responses, it was impossible to directly incorporate all of their insights into the text. We did, however, learn a great deal from each engagement.

Our thought collective, like most others, has several layers. The group that truly shaped this work lived and learned together at R. Earle Davis Elementary School in South Carolina. We thank Sandra Pees, the class tutor, for her constant diligence, observations, and friendship. We can think of no finer educator or friend to children. David Whitin, a colleague from the University of South Carolina and a fellow teacher-researcher, constantly reminded us what was really important and lived his model at the university and in the elementary classroom. Tom Warren and Carol Martig were truly supportive administrators whose primary concerns were with the students in their charge. They exemplified what administrators ought to be. Finally, the six year olds in the transition classroom taught us the most significant lessons.

Jane Curran and Rona Smith helped us refine our work. They were always cheerful, patient, and insightful. Michael Spooner helped in numerous ways. He actually had a vision for this text before we did. He was constantly supportive throughout the entire process. Michael is truly connected to teachers and children and has a lovely way of helping his authors create texts to meet their needs and interests. We are particularly grateful for his support when times were tough.

There are always a few people who are not directly connected to a book but who are distant teachers. Daniel Baron was an early mentor who taught a lifetime of lessons. And there are those who do not even know us. Tim O'Keefe would like to acknowledge Dr. Seuss for teaching him how to read.

Finally, we would like to thank the teachers and children who were not satisfied with what was typical. They helped us see what was possible.

Introduction

Timothy O'Keefe

I have always considered myself a whole language teacher. In 1977, I took a general language arts methods course from Jerome Harste at Indiana University. The reading, reflections, and discussions from that class not only altered how I felt about language arts instruction, but they changed my feelings toward all instruction. My new understandings led me to raise questions in all of my subsequent courses concerning the relevance of instruction, the social nature of learning, the importance of context, trusting students as learners, authentic communication, and risk taking. In short, my eyes were fitted with a new set of lenses through which to view education.

Through many varied teaching experiences—from preschool through grade six, in team-teaching situations to self-contained classrooms to pull-out programs for basic skill instruction—I have always emphasized meaningful reading and writing and the sharing of ideas and discoveries as the core of my curriculum. The classroom viewed in this book is a small, self-contained class of young children considered "at risk," but I firmly believe that the whole language philosophy works well for all ages and populations, whether they are grouped by ability or grouped heterogeneously. This only makes sense, given that the whole language philosophy emerged from research focusing on how children learn; in turn, whole language teachers teach in ways that are consistent with how children learn.

Of course, how whole language is implemented varies as much as the teachers, students, and settings. In this text, I have tried to show and tell how it worked for me during one year. Thus the book is not intended to be a "how-to" book, but rather, it provides a glimpse of a classroom where meaning was the essence of the curriculum. While graphophonemic relationships are highlighted, I hope that it is obvious that I constantly made an effort to get children to focus on the multiple cue systems available to them, for no cue system by itself is sufficient for effective communication. To the students in my class, letter sounds were only one way of supporting the meaning-making process, and it only worked when used in concert with other cue systems. In no way do I think that graphophonemics is more important than other cue systems, but given the recent controversy surrounding the use of phonics (as demonstrated in issues of *Language Arts* and *The Reading Teacher*), I hope that this text may serve as a catalyst for further exploration into how sound-symbol relationships may be learned in a whole language classroom, and that it may answer questions about how phonics may be put into its proper perspective.

There are several important studies which allow teachers to explore the relationship between whole language and the use of various cue systems (particularly graphophonemics). As I read and reflect upon other research projects with a similar focus (Church and Newman 1985; DeFord 1981; DeLawter 1985; Freppon and Dahl 1991; Mills and Clyde 1991; Stice and Bertrand 1989; Willert and Kamii 1985), I am struck by the fact that they often confirm insights that I have gained from watching my own children carefully. While these studies each make unique contributions to the field, the essence of their findings rings true to me as a classroom teacher. I find them especially useful because they help me better understand my own students' learning. I can translate their findings into future instructional decisions.

The question may arise as to how we can be sure to cover all of the graphophonemic information that children need as they emerge into the world of literacy. I have found that by allowing children to use what they know about print to create and test new hypotheses, and to share what they know in an atmosphere designed to encourage social interaction (as opposed to starting everyone off with instruction arbitrarily conceived of as "beginning language instruction"), the children learn what *they need to learn* and do well in teaching their peers about their newfound insights. Instead of covering an externally mandated language arts curriculum, the children and I uncovered important aspects about language that I believe assisted them in communicating effectively about topics of interest to them—including knowledge of sound-symbol relationships. I have further found that this most often surpasses the expectations of textbooks that teach phonics in a decontextualized manner in which application to authentic communication is much more difficult and abstract.

One essential characteristic of the curriculum in my classroom is that I consider myself to be a teacher-researcher. The extensive data collection and analysis that I use (videotapes and audiotapes, collecting written language samples over time, field notes with anecdotes and language stories, and written communication with parents) constantly inform my decisions concerning the classroom. By watching and listening to my students, I feel that I can better make decisions concerning what is best for them as learners and teachers themselves. The children in my class see that I am a learner and know that I am interested in how learning takes place. They notice that I am learning along with them and often show this by assisting me in my data collection. They can often detect when something is interesting to me, and voluntarily bring my clipboard with field notes. "Mr. O'Keefe, you'd better come here. This is *interesting!*" has been said in many different ways, indicating to me that these students also see me as a student. This too encourages reflection on their part, for I assume that an interaction or observation must be exciting to them if they believe it is so for me.

By being a teacher-researcher, I am not simply implementing theory in my classroom; I am generating theory through teaching. The classroom is constantly evolving as we follow new directions based on the current interests of the children and myself. Our class looks and feels different each year—reflecting our different intrigues and questions (see, for example, "A Day with Dinosaurs" in Mills and Clyde 1990; Whitin, Mills, and O'Keefe 1990).

The process of writing about and presenting what I have learned has made me more watchful and aware of the potential of whole language. Not only does writing allow me to share what I already know, but it helps me to look more closely at my teaching and children's learning, which, in turn, leads me to new understandings and questions.

Much energy and time go into planning, record keeping, data collection and evaluation, and analysis in this kind of classroom. However, the energy it takes to make the class work is, at the same time, revitalizing. Each year presents new curiosities and areas to explore with the incoming group of students. Each year is unique and startling in its potential for learning. Teachers who have become or continue to be learners do not turn back. They listen to their students' voices.

I hope that the children's voices come through in this volume. Children's reflections are very powerful tools when trying to understand the learning process. By showing their writing and, I hope, by allowing them to demonstrate their growth and development, this text is an attempt to let these children be our teachers.

2 Highlighting the Role of Graphophonemics on a Typical Day

In this chapter, we relive a typical day in April 1990. The description weaves the events together in a manner that illustrates the connectedness of experiences while featuring the rich opportunities that the children have to construct and share insights about letter-sound relationships. It is important to remember that we have not isolated graphophonemics from the rest of the day, but have highlighted it in such a way as to make it visible and understandable. Readers will be introduced to Tony, Jessica, and Kareem in this chapter and will follow these children through the typical day. Chapter 3 will focus on just these three children by exploring their growth over the year.

Routine Activities

As the day begins, Tim is busy writing the morning business on the board:

- Surveys during free choice time
- Menu
- Stick calendar
- Journal Sharing—Stephen, Nikki, and Charles
- Kareem's reading strategy

This list will guide the discussion at the first meeting this morning. As Tim writes, the children enter the classroom and put their book bags in their cubbies. Most of them are continuing conversations that began on the bus or playground. A familiar hum begins to fill the room. It is good noise; some children laugh with delight while others are seriously enthralled by their topics. Tim and his teaching assistant, Sandra Pees, join in the conversations. They are interested in the children's stories as a source of important insights about the children's lives and interests. Such knowledge is often used when making daily plans.

During this time, the children also sign in. They have been writing their names in the attendance journal (see Figure 2) since

Figure 2
Class attendance journal.

the first day of school. Tim uses this document to keep track of student attendance and to trace the development of the children's writing over time. The journal provides concrete evidence for Tim, the parents, and, most importantly, the children. They enjoy looking back at their signatures and discussing how they used to write. By now, they can easily read each other's names. Earlier in the year, rich, fruitful discussions ensued around letters and sounds in children's names. Tim celebrates children's language discoveries through class strategy-sharing discussions:

> Chiquita and Charles both have the letters *ch* at the beginning of their names.
>
> Justin noticed that *O'Keefe* has two *e*'s, like in Kareem's name. Then he looked around the room and saw the color words collages. He added *green* to his list of words that have two *e*'s together.
>
> Amanda noticed that she, Justin, and Vania all have *r*'s in their last names.

The children enjoyed comparing and contrasting the letters and sounds in each other's names so much that Tim created a class game from their observations. He would say, for example, "I am thinking of a name that begins with a *c*." The children would then immediately generate all of the possibilities. Tim would next refine his clue by naming the second letter, *h*. This, of course, reduced the first list. He would then add another letter, talking about the corresponding sound each time. Soon the children guessed the name and helped him complete the spelling.

Numerous insights about letter-sound relationships emerged during this and other games, and children often played these games independently or in small groups during free choice time. Tim attributes the success of this particular game to the fact that he followed the children's lead when creating it. He is always looking for ways to connect the children's personal knowledge and interests to concepts. This game built on their interest in names, while it helped them understand the consistencies and inconsistencies of sound-symbol relationships.

Free Choice Time

After signing in, the children spend the next twenty minutes engaged in free choice time. Yesterday, Tim conducted a survey to find out what his students like to do best on the playground. Now he collaborates with Amanda to "show" the results using pictures. Several children are building with blocks, two are reading Bill Martin stories at the listening center, three children are painting at the easel, one child is completing a challenging new puzzle, and a few are continuing their work on drafts of stories they intend to publish this week. At 8:20 a.m., Tim picks up his guitar and begins playing the familiar clean-up music. The children know that they need to clean up their materials and to meet him at the front of the class by the end of the song.

First Class Gathering

As the children settle into their positions on the floor, Tim asks for song requests. Hands shoot up in the air. "ABC Blues," a song that Tim wrote, is the first choice this morning. Although Tim does not teach the alphabet in isolation, he finds that the children use it daily through such songs as "ABC Blues" and "ABC Rock" (from *We All Live Together,* 1975, Young Heart Records, Los Angeles). Earlier in the year, the children often chose to write the alphabet in their journals, singing one of these songs while composing. By now they have come to value the role of letters as useful tools that help them construct genuine messages. Today, after singing several other class favorites—"Tools Was a Baby Rabbit," "Walking through the Park," and "Sing a Rainbow"—Tim reminds the children that he has written the songs on chart paper. He mentions them as potential reading material during quiet reading time.

"The first item on our agenda this morning is . . . ," Tim pauses to allow the children to read his message. Kareem reads, "Surveys during free choice time." Tim thanks Kareem for reading and then proceeds to explain the meaning of this agenda item. He has noticed that many children are conducting surveys during writing workshop time. Because they have to interrupt their classmates in order to gather their information, Tim would like to restrict surveys to free choice time. Tim suggests that interruptions often make it difficult to concentrate on writing. He reminds the children that they have approximately twenty minutes in the morning and another twenty minutes each afternoon during their free choice time. Some children are disappointed, but they understand that they will need to save the surveys for a particular time of day.

"Menu!" the children exclaim as Tim uses the pointer to address the next item of business. Tim reads the menu for lunch today. Some children respond positively, while others make faces that portray a dislike for the selection.

"Stick calendar," they all read in chorus.

Tim comments, "Yesterday we had one ten and eight ones." Hands shoot up in the air. "Amanda, what should we do today?"

"Add another stick, so one ten and nine ones. Tomorrow we get to bundle them up." Amanda is right. Every time a group of ten ones is collected, the popsicle sticks are bound together with a rubber band and placed in the tens bag. Two simple clear plastic bags labeled *tens* and *ones* help the children learn about place value through daily calendar changes. Tim creates strategies like this in order to weave mathematical insights into the fabric of the day.

Returning to the daily business, Tim announces, "Stephen, Nikki, and Charles all get to share journals today if they want. Also, several children are almost ready to publish their books. If you finish during quiet writing time today, you may also share your work." Before dismissing the children for the writing workshop, Tim tells them, "I would like to share a strategy I noticed Kareem use yesterday during writing time." Tim continues, "Kareem wrote me a message. He wrote, 'How are you today? I hope you feel fine.' " Tim writes Kareem's message on the board. Then he comments, "Of course, I wrote him a message back. I wrote, 'I like your sweater. It has a *v* on it.' " Tim writes his message under Kareem's. "When Kareem read it, he came to a word he didn't know. Kareem, tell us what you did."

"I didn't know *sweater* so I skipped it, and when I got to the part that says it has a *v* on it, I knew it was *sweater*," Kareem answers matter-of-factly.

Tim responds, "That was a good strategy. When you come to a word you don't know, sometimes it helps to skip it, like Kareem did, try to make sense by looking at the rest of the sentence, and then just go back."

Strategy-sharing sessions such as these are used to publicly recognize the children's effective reading and writing strategies. Tim invites children to share strategies in order to validate their thinking and to provide their young colleagues with opportunities to try out new strategies on their own.

Writing Workshop

As Tim dismisses the group, he reminds them about the new survey rule. The children move to their cubbies to get their journals or storybooks-in-progress. They select a spot at one of the four tables and begin discussing their plans.

"I'm going to write about my cat and dog story," Nikki remarks softly.

Jason responds, "I'm working on my Ninja Turtles book."

Tim finds a chair by Amanda. He wants to help her complete the playground project this morning, since he plans to use the data for a mathematics project in the afternoon.

The children begin working on their writing. Children who want to write messages for the message board join Sandra at her table. Several boys have developed a support group and choose to work together during writing time. In the group, they help each other with ideas for their writing. A few children find quiet spots away from the group for concentration.

Tim consistently chooses to work on projects during this time, while simultaneously supporting his students. Children often come to his table to share their current drafts. Vania wants to read her newly published book. She just finished it and wants to read it to Tim before sharing it with the rest of the class. Tim listens intently as she reads. "Once upon a time there was a cat and a dog and they saw a snake. And then the dog ate the cat and the cat ate the . . . Mr. O'Keefe, what's that word?"

Tim rereads her text, hoping that the flow of the language (syntax) in combination with the meaning of her story (semantics) will signal the word she is concerned about. "And then the dog ate the cat and the cat ate the s . . ."

"Snake!" responds Vania confidently. She continues reading. When pausing a second time, she glances at Tim for help.

This time he responds differently: "Tell me what your story is about. What happened after the cat ate the snake?" This nudge is all she needs to keep going.

Today is Tony's turn to write the message for the class calendar. He takes the small rectangular sheet of colored paper from the calendar bulletin board and begins writing. The class calendar is much like a class learning log because the children take turns recording important classroom events and personal experiences.

They bind the cards into a class book at the end of every month. Like many of the children, Tony decides to write about something on which he is currently working. Tim pauses and listens to Tony read: "I'm making a book."

Tim often asks the children to reflect on their own learning. Because this particular text is brief, he asks Tony to share his spelling strategies. "How did you know to write *I'm* like that?" The children realize that such queries are authentic. Tim truly wants to understand the reading and writing strategies they use. He will make future instructional decisions based on such data.

Tony explains, "I just learned that you had an apostrophe in your name, and I already knew how to write *IM*, and I remembered it started with a capital and then a lower case." Tim repeats what Tony has said. Tony adds, "I memorized how to write *I'm* from my brother's math book."

Tim continues the conversation: "How did you know how to write *making*?" which Tony wrote as *macking*.

Tony responds, "I've seen you put *ck* on the end of words. Then I just wrote the *m* and the *a* and *ing*," showing a sensitivity to common letter patterns in words in combination with knowledge of sound-symbol relationships.

"How did you know the *ing*?" asks Tim.

"You taught me that they go together," answers Tony.

"Thank you, Tony," says Tim. "May I share some of your strategies during gathering?"

Tony replies, "Sure." Tony's explanation highlights how he uses multiple strategies to construct and share meaning. He accesses strategies that are most appropriate for various words and different parts of words.

Megan approaches Tim next. She wants to know if her story makes sense so far. She reads, "One time there was a book. All the people read the book." She looks at her teacher for feedback.

Tim looks at Tony and Paul. "Does that make sense?" They both nod their heads. Tim confirms their opinion by stating, "Sounds good to me."

A question arises: "What book?"

Megan replies, "Vania's book."

"That might be good information for your reader," suggests Tim.

Megan returns to her table armed with confidence in her current text and an idea to develop further for her readers.

Tony decides to stay at this table to help Amanda with the playground project. Meanwhile, Paul has been busily writing and is now ready to share. As Paul begins reading to Tim, Tim takes notes to help him with future editing. "The frog was swimming," reads Paul. "The snake was swimming too. He grabbed the frog. Then the turtle killed the snake. And then the turtle tried to tell the frog. But the frog got the turtle. The frog lived happily ever after."

Tony glances at Paul's text and comments: "Some kids use one letter for a word. See, there are some words in there where he just put single letters by themselves; I bet a lot of kids write like that when they start writing, even me." Looking at Tim, he adds, "I bet you did, too."

Amanda chimes in, "Yeah, even Kareem." Tim is delighted that they are reflecting on intentionality and the process of learning to write.

"No, I don't think Kareem or Stephen did," Tony reacts.

Tim asks, "Do you think they started with whole words?"

Everyone responds in harmony, "Nah!"

Tim continues the discussion by asking, "How do you think they got started?"

Tony thinks about his friend's strategies. "I only know Kareem sounds his words out."

Amanda adds, "By his brain."

Tim follows up on Tony's assessment, inquiring, "What do you mean?"

"That's what I sometimes hear Kareem do when he is reading. I can hear him sounding out the letters sometimes when he is reading."

"Yeah, and there are other things he does too—like that strategy he shared this morning," adds the teacher. "He wasn't sounding out at all. He just figured out what it meant. He had it make sense." Tim does not downplay Tony's idea, but emphasizes the strategic nature of Kareem's reading and focuses on the importance of "making sense."

As quiet writing time draws to a close, Tim reminds the children to return all of their works-in-progress to their cubbies and asks them to assemble for gathering time. Stephen and Charles keep their journals because they plan to share what they have written with the class.

Sharing Time   Tim reads Stephen's name from the board, and Stephen reaches for the microphone. Tim encourages the children to read into the microphone that is connected to the record player. He has found that sharing time is enhanced because the children with soft voices can be heard, and using the microphone formalizes the importance of this time of day.

Stephen begins reading his latest published book: "Raphael said, 'Michaelangelo, go get Leonardo. What do you want? And then let's get our things to fight.' Raphael got one turtle and then they beat Shredder up. The end."

The children applaud, and Charles makes his way to the front of the group. Stephen passes the microphone to Charles, who begins reading, "Leonardo beat up Bee Bop." He starts to turn the page, but the children interrupt him. "Let's see the pictures!" they exclaim, showing that they value the illustrations. As Charles slowly moves the book across the group, Tim responds, "Very nice pictures, Charles."

After Charles finishes reading, it is Vania's turn. She begins by reading the title of her story, "The Cat and the Dog." She continues: "Once upon a time there was a cat and a dog. And they saw a man." She pauses to show the illustrations. "And then the dog and the cat ate the snake and the dog ate the flea." The children break into spontaneous applause when she is finished.

Tim asks, "Do you have something written on the back of your book?" Vania nods. "Could you read it to us?"

"Vania, girl, 6, Mr. O'Keefe."

Tim reacts warmly. "That says it all. She is sharing biographical information. She is writing about herself," he says, connecting Vania's idea to professionally published texts.

Tim concludes writing-sharing time by asking Tony to read aloud his calendar card. He and Tony talk about Tony's writing strategies. Tony holds his calendar card up so his friends can see the text, reading, "I'm making a book." The calendar cards portray each child's curricular interests. This news reflects what Tony values.

Tim capitalizes on one of Tony's insights about language. Talking to the group, he explains, "It was really interesting when Tony was writing *I'm*. He was writing it like this." Tim writes an exact transcription on the board. "I asked him how he remembered to write the apostrophe. He said he remembered I had an apostrophe in my name, and had seen the word *I'm* in his brother's math book," he says, emphasizing the connections Tony made between prior reading experiences and his current text.

Tony adds, "I had a capital because it is the first letter in the sentence and then used a small *m*," reminding his friends what he knows about capital letters.

Recess is next. Tim asks Chiquita to name the categories. She moves to the front of the class and begins dismissing her friends according to their clothing. "If you are wearing red you may line up. If you are wearing white tennis shoes . . ." Children play a key role in the organization and management of the curriculum.

Recess

Tim enjoys recess as much as the children do. Today he assists with the jump rope activities. Several children have been challenging themselves and charting their growth on graph paper. They all celebrate together when one of their friends increases his or her personal best score.

Reading a Chapter Book

After recess, Tim continues reading a chapter book entitled *Rabbit Hill* by Robert Lawson (Viking Press, 1944). "We are beginning a new chapter today. Let's think about what has happened so far." After a short conversation about events and characters, Tim gets ready to read. "Okay, page 56, Uncle decided he was going to take a bath."

Several children recall this section and shout, "Kids, you may never hear me say that word."

Tim responds by rereading this section to acknowledge their point: ". . . you may never hear me speak these words again in your whole life. Georgie—*I'm goin' to take me a bath!*" Next he reads the chapter title and continues reading, "Porkey Sits Tight. The next few days saw great doings on the Hill. In fact there was so much going on that Father was fairly worn out . . ." (61).

Quiet Reading Time

A number of children go to the class library and select published children's literature. Four children decide to read newly published books by their colleagues, while three others sit down at the listening center and begin discussing which book and tape they want. Two children find their favorite predictable big books and lay them on the floor. They are immediately joined by three more children who want to read with them. There is a moment of confusion as the children decide who will be in charge of the pointer. They all enjoy using the "space tubes" or "magic wands" as pointers and are very conscientious about this responsibility. The pointer reflects the rhythm of the language as they read. As the children settle into their texts in various locations in the room, a hum fills the air. They are careful not to disturb their neighbors, but many enjoy reading together, and so quiet reading time is not really quiet. Tim moves about the room to support his readers and to listen to their miscues (K. Goodman 1967). He can tell a great deal about their reading strategies by listening in on their informal reading. Ray, a new child in the class, notices that his name is embedded in the word *crayons*. Tim acknowledges this word-within-word observation and asks him to remember to share his insight with the class.

Tim sits down next to Vania. She continues reading as if she doesn't even realize her teacher is there. She reads and reads before acknowledging his presence. She is in the midst of a Dr.

Seuss book, *One Fish, Two Fish, Red Fish, Blue Fish* (Random House, 1960), when she reads *Zam* for *Zans*. She immediately self-corrects the miscue, looks to her teacher, and explains, "I changed this word [*Zans*] to my brother's name [*Zam*]."

Tim tells her that he can see why she did that. "They are almost alike because they both begin with *z* and *a*." Tim notes that Vania is using multiple cue systems. Her initial attempt reflects use of letter-sound relationships and shape or word configuration cues. She then uses syntactic and semantic cues to self-correct a miscue. The children continue reading while Tim and Sandra ask individuals to wash their hands in preparation for lunch. At 11:00 a.m. they all put their books away and head for the cafeteria.

Mathematics: Playground Stories

After lunch Tim introduces a potential mathematics project. He has found that children often choose to participate in formal invitations created in response to students' needs and interests. Additionally, they often extend and revise invitations to meet their own needs when pursuing such endeavors independently. He begins by inviting Kareem to share the survey he conducted the day before. Kareem asked his friends, "Do you like football or swings or frisbee? You can sign up for two." Kareem shows the class his survey.

"Why did you let people pick two?" Tim asks.

" 'Cause they would probably like it" is Kareem's matter-of-fact reply, which indicates a sensitivity to his audience. He is right; most of the children enjoy more than one playground activity. In fact, several children commented that their favorites were not listed. Knowing this, Tim addressed such concerns in his survey.

Tim tells the group that he liked Kareem's survey idea so much that he conducted one like it. He frequently follows the children's lead in order to validate their ideas and to demonstrate flexible ways to pose questions. Tim's survey was also about playground activities, but he left the choices completely open. He simply asked what the children liked to do on the playground and told them they could choose whatever they wanted. Then he created categories for his survey as ideas were generated. He found that several children chose frisbee, some said swings, one decided on kickball, and another selected football. Megan responded, "Walk around"; Jessica said she liked running; Amanda and Vania said they loved jumping rope.

Tim asks Amanda to share with the class the visual representation that she made of the data (see Figure 3). They talk about the creation of the picture with the class. Amanda has drawn a frisbee for all the children who selected frisbee as their favorite activity, and put their names inside. Next she drew a purple ball

Figure 3
Amanda's visual represen-
tation of survey data,
19 April 1990.

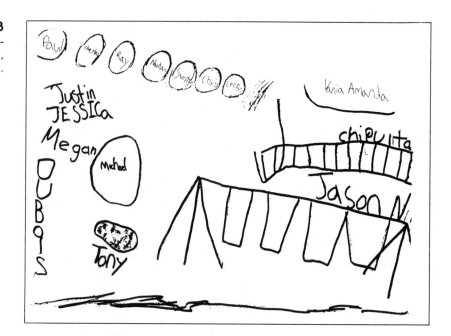

for kickball and put Michael's name inside it. She continued putting names in or close to the pictures of the choices children made.
She had not been sure how to depict walking and running because
there was not a specific physical object to associate with either
activity. With a little help from her friends, she decided to write
their names sideways for running, because "running goes sideways," and vertically for walking, because "walking goes up and
down." Through conversation the children are applauded for their
interesting problem-solving strategies. Tim emphasizes how challenging it was to represent or "show" walking and running. Children conclude the sharing session by discussing several mathematical stories about the survey that were written during free choice
time.

Tim begins the discussion using Heidi's story: "Heidi found
out that Nikki, Justin, and Chris like to play frisbee, so she cut out
their pictures and made pictures of them throwing the frisbee. Paul
and Michael like football, so she made them playing football in the
corner. She used speech bubbles to let us know what they were
saying and used numbers in her story. The equation is to help us
understand what is happening. 'Three kids are playing frisbee.
Nikki is throwing it to Justin and Chris. Two kids are playing
football. 3 (frisbee) + 2 (football) = 5 (kids playing).' "

The children are intrigued with the idea of using their own
photographs in the stories. Tim answers a few questions and lis-

tens as the children begin talking about making their own playground stories. He then extends an invitation: "I made copies of everyone's pictures so that you could use them to make your own playground story. You could use pictures of your friends, art, writing, and mathematics to represent your ideas."

Numerous children begin their stories. Several draw pictures first and then begin to write about the characters. Tony talks his way through his plans: "Mr. O'Keefe is going to be throwing the frisbee, and Derrick can't catch it. He is little so I should have him jump up." His final text is similar: "Mr. O'Keefe threw the frisbee, and I caught it. Justin jumped up. Derrick was too small. I was blocking Derrick."

Heidi soon notices the detail in Tony's drawings (see Figure 4) and shares this with the group: "Look what Tony did, you guys. He noticed that Mr. O'Keefe has a tie on in his picture and so he extended the tie using art. You know the other thing he did that is interesting? Mr. O'Keefe is pretty tall, and Derrick is pretty short." Turning to Tony, she comments, "That was really authentic the way you drew Derrick to be as tall as Mr. O'Keefe's waist. We have been measuring our heights a lot in here, and your picture is a good way to show it."

LeeAnn interrupts to explain how she knows $5 + 3 = 8$. "I have it in my head. And then I go 5" (holding five fingers up on her left hand) "and then 6, 7, 8" (adding three fingers by lifting them on her right hand).

Heidi confirms LeeAnn's strategy: "She knows $5 + 3 = 8$ in her head, but she checks herself by starting with the largest number (5) and adding three more (6, 7, 8). Good strategy."

Tim is working at another table with Jessica, Paul, Vania, and Charles. Michael taps Tim on the shoulder to get feedback about his current illustrations. Jessica looks too and comments, "That's pretty, Michael."

"Thank you Jessica. That was nice to say," responds Tim warmly.

Michael explains, "They're climbing on the monkey bars."

"See if you can show me what you mean using an equation," Tim suggests, hoping Michael will complement and extend the meaning of his illustrations using mathematics.

Paul is immersed in his own work and seems to be oblivious to this conversation. He is quite delighted with his creation. Talking to himself, he exclaims, "Look how high Derrick is jumping! Woooow!"

Charles has begun with an equation and shares it with Tim, who asks, "Tell me what your numbers mean."

Figure 4
Tony's playground story,
19 April 1990.

"There were four people and two went away, so 4 − 2 = 2."
Tim nods in confirmation, and Charles continues working.

Tim finally begins working on his own playground creation
and discusses his plans with children at his table. "I have four kids
playing jump rope. What could four other kids do?"

They respond in unison, "Walking; they could race."

"I like that," Tim responds to the racing suggestion. "I will
have all of the kids at this table running in a race. I think I'll put
Vania in the front. She's pretty fast." He continues making a connection between this experience and life on the playground.

Paul finishes his first story and wants to begin another one.
Tim notices that it takes Paul a great deal of time simply to cut out
the photos, so he offers his assistance. Tim prefers to have Paul
spend time concentrating on his story rather than cutting out photos. "Paul, I will help you cut out pictures. Who would you like?"

"Charles, Jason, and Tony," Paul replies as he embarks on
another creation.

It is interesting to note how stories can be told using language, art, and mathematics. Each form of communication tells the
story in a unique way. Many children illustrate the text first and
then begin writing about the characters. Others begin with an
equation and create narratives through art and writing that complement and extend the meaning embedded in their numerical
stories. Because children are using written language to construct
and share meaning, grapheme-phoneme relationships play a key

role in the experience. The children all rely on their knowledge about language to communicate their ideas. Some children have a well-developed repertoire of words they spell conventionally and use them in conjunction with invented spellings to portray their meanings. Other children primarily call upon their knowledge of sound-symbol relationships to write what they mean, not simply what they can spell. As in all aspects of language learning, these children are expanding and refining their understanding of sound-symbol relationships while using language to learn and to communicate. Hence, this experience reveals the children's evolving understanding of mathematics, as well as their developing control of language.

Pen Pal Letters

Although this is a typical day, it is important to note the fact that this is a typical Thursday. Thursdays have become "pen pal letter days" in an effort to maintain continuous, predictable communication with the children's writing partners. Tim works with small groups during this time of day the rest of the week. The children select a study group topic and conduct research in this area. They read, write, conduct experiments, and so on while investigating a self-selected topic, such as endangered species. They always conclude their projects by sharing what they have learned with the rest of the class. They "show" what they have learned by composing songs, writing plays or books, or creating video productions, paintings, or sculptures. Tim encourages the children to choose a form of communication that will most effectively help them present the essence of their learning.

Tim announces the final activity for the day by reading another book to the class, *Manners: Notes and Letters* by A. Tharee (Grolier, 1988): "I found a new series of books in the library. They are all about manners. And even though that may not sound like an interesting topic, this one has a lot of good ideas for us to think about when we write our pen pal letters." Tim begins reading the section in the book in which a child is writing a thank-you card and composes two drafts before completing the note. In the first draft, he forgets to include information about the present he received. The second draft is much more detailed and personally meaningful. As the story continues, the little boy becomes concerned about spelling, stating, "I don't know how to spell it right." The mother replies, "That's ok, do it the best you can. The most important thing is not that you spelled exactly right, the most important thing is that you spelled by yourself."

Tim draws a connection between the story and the children's own letters: "Just like our pen pal letters. We can't tell you what to say—you have to figure that out on your own. The most important part is not getting everything spelled right, but writing exactly what you want to say. These are very important letters because this is the last time you will write to your pen pal before the pen pal party."

The children begin wiggling with excitement. They have been corresponding with undergraduate students from the University of South Carolina for four months. Each week they write and receive a letter. The project gives the children an authentic reason for writing and an audience who truly cares about them. The adults learn how to support children's writing growth and how to track an individual child's progress. They come to realize the importance of making personal connections with children. While they are naturally teachers in this context, they are also learners, friends, and colleagues.

The thrill of receiving a letter from their special friends pervades the room. As Tim passes out the letters, the children begin reading them. Vania opens her envelope. "A picture, a picture," she exclaims, speaking directly to a small group of friends. "I got a picture!"

Kareem responds enthusiastically, "Look. Mine got a baby!" Megan grabs it from his hand and examines it closely. "Don't put dirty hands on it!" he exclaims as he shows his friends how to hold photographs by the edge.

Some children read the letters independently, while others find a friend or adult to help them. Michael begins posing questions for his pen pal. "Do you like fish? Do you like shrimp?" he writes, slowly articulating the last word and spelling it *shp*.

Tony and LeeAnn begin reading a letter together. They read in concert until Tony gets stuck. "What's this word?" he asks as Tim walks by.

"Try Kareem's strategy," Tim suggests, "just skip it."

Tony starts over. "Tony, Hi!" he reads. "How are you doing? I'm fine. The Navy ship sounds *iii-xxx . . .*" He looks up at his teacher.

"That line means she divided the word," Tim remarks, pointing to the word *exciting*, which is hyphenated after the *x*. "She did that because she ran out of room."

Tony is a child who talks his way through writing, thus making his thinking visible. When he wants to write *pen pal*, he writes *pen* fluently, but pauses before he writes *pal*, articulating "*ppp-aa-ll*" as he composes.

While Tony writes, LeeAnn is reading the letter from her pen pal and miscues. She substitutes "valentine" for *vacation*. Because it does not make sense, she becomes frustrated. Knowing that LeeAnn is a child who gives up easily, Tim gives direct assistance: "*Vacation*. I know why you probably said 'valentine' because they both start with a *v*." Tim also realizes that the words are graphically similar as they have similar configurations of letters and similar lengths. Nonetheless, he wants LeeAnn to keep going—to focus on what would make sense and to rely less on within-word cues. LeeAnn rereads her letter with confidence this time.

Tony continues composing, reading his text outloud as he goes (see Figure 5). "It looks like you got a ring. Can you send me another letter on the computer? I will keep sending you some." He pauses and remarks, "What did she ask me about Jessica?" He unfolds his letter again and reads until he finds his pen pal's question. "Oh yeah," he remarks as he begins writing a specific response to her question. "No, Jessica [his girlfriend] can't come [to the party]. I can't wait for the pen pal party. It will be ever . . ." He pauses trying to remember what he wanted to say and realizes he skipped a line. "[You] will be my very best pen pal I ever met, pen pal. Love, Tony."

It is clear that Tony is a reader who attends to spelling during the reading and writing process. He spells familiar words conventionally and uses what he knows about language to construct unfamiliar words. A close look at his decisions reveals logical, systematic, and rule-governed thinking and a sophisticated understanding of sound-symbol relationships. The important thing, however, as Tim mentioned when reading the book about letter writing, is that Tony writes what he means, not simply what he can spell. Therefore, his texts reflect his thoughts. Tony's classmates demonstrate these concepts as well. Jessica, for example, waits to read her letter aloud (see Figure 6) until she is finished writing: "Dear Aimee, How are you? I'm fine. How are you? It was my birthday and she is my friend! I have a basket full of candy. I ate some. Yes, I did get new shoes! Yes, I like *Stuart Little!*"

Stephen is anxious to read his letter aloud, even though he is mad at his pen pal because she did not send him a letter this week. Stephen confronts her and then continues writing as usual: "Dear Sara, Why did [didn't] you give me a letter? Can you bring me a priz for me? Do you like pen pal partys? Your pen pal, Stephen."

Amanda wants Tim's feedback before sealing her envelope. She reads her letter. "Dear Jamie, Why didn't you send me a letter? Have a Happy Easter. P.S. I'll be happy to see you when we meet. You are pretty. I love you."

Tim comments, "I'm glad you put a postscript."

Figure 5
Tony's letter to his pen pal,
19 April 1990.

When Stephen leans over to ask how to spell *sister*, Kareem jumps up and states, "I know how to spell it. I saw it in a book." Kareem gets up to find the book. Tim smiles and lets Kareem teach Stephen how to spell the word. Even more importantly, Kareem is showing Stephen an effective strategy, finding words in familiar texts.

As the children complete their letters, they place them in the official USC envelope and begin gathering together their belongings for the ride home. It has been a good day, a typically good day, for the teacher and for the children.

Reflecting on Teaching and Learning

Anyone who has visited a whole language classroom realizes that the learning environment is richly complex. The complexity does not result in chaos, but instead reveals a flexible curricular structure that encourages all of the participants to function as teachers and learners. Consequently, the curriculum is constantly shaped and reshaped with each new insight or question. The teacher consistently attends to what the children are learning and how the teaching is either enhancing or restricting learning. The teacher has a solid understanding of the language-learning process and uses this information to guide his or her planning and responses to the children's thinking. However, because learning in whole language classrooms is so richly contextualized, significant learning incidents are often overlooked. To emphasize the teaching strategies that

Figure 6
Jessica's letter to her pen pal, 19 April 1990.

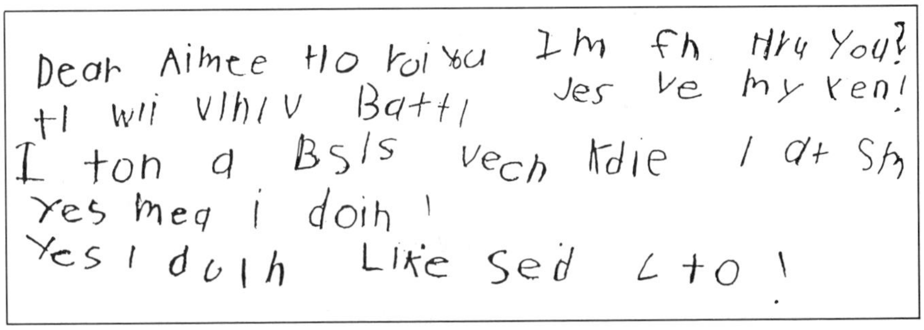
Dear Aimee Hlo Hoi you I'm fn Hru You?
tl wil vlhlv Battl Jes ve my ken!
I ton a Bsls vech kdie I at Sh
yes meq i doih !
Yes I doih Like Sed L to !

most effectively supported the learning of various reading-writing strategies and language concepts on this particular day, we conclude with a chart (see Table 1) highlighting the language learning during our typical day in Tim's classroom.

Sign-in Journal. The journal featured student attendance patterns and documented the children's development over time in their ability to write their names. It also served as a forum for children to learn about the letters and sounds in their friends' names. Children made frequent observations about similarities in names, such as: "*Charles* and *Chiquita* both begin with the letters *ch*"; "*O'Keefe* has two *e*'s like Kareem's name and *green*"; "Amanda, Justin, and Vania all have *r*'s in their last names." The children frequently used data from this journal to figure out new spellings. They did so by making connections between letter patterns in their friends' names and other words.

Name Game. Tim devised a game that encouraged the children to make predictions using their knowledge of letter-sound relationships in conjunction with their friends' names. They connected their personal knowledge and interests with graphophonemic concepts by uncovering consistencies and inconsistencies in language.

"ABC Blues" and "ABC Rock." Children learned the alphabet in the context of two popular class songs. Children often referred to the class-made alphabet cards above the chalkboard while playing "air guitar" and singing in rhythm to the teacher's guitar.

Class Strategy-Sharing Sessions. The teacher shared an effective reading strategy he saw Kareem use. Kareem skipped the word *sweater* when reading his teacher's message and then went back to self-correct his reading when he read the clue embedded in the sentence "It has a *v* on it." Kareem's sweater did in fact have a large *v* on the front of it, and Kareem strategically used this information to make sense of the sentence and to figure out the word *sweater*.

Table 1
A Summary of Reading-
Writing Strategies and
Language Concepts

Curricular Structure	Language Concepts and Strategies
Attendance Journal	Learning letters and their corresponding sounds in children's names.
Name Game	Predictions about class names; constructing knowledge about consistencies and inconsistencies in grapheme-phoneme relationships.
"ABC Blues" and "ABC Rock"	Naming and recognizing letters in alphabetical order.
Class Strategy-Sharing Sessions	Reading strategy: skip a word that you are unsure of and come back to it once you read the rest of the sentence and can make a logical prediction.
Supporting Readers	Reading strategy: use all cue systems (syntax, semantics, and graphophonemics) in concert to construct meaning.
Reflecting on Writing Strategies	Form develops through functional use; children learn about language while using language to communicate and to learn. Contractions have an apostrophe. Words such as *I'm* and *I'll* always begin with a capital letter. Use visual memory from reading when spelling. Certain letter combinations are common in the English language, e.g., *ck* and *ing*. Listen for sounds in words when spelling new words.
Editing for Publication	Young writers sometimes use one key letter to represent a word.
Informal Strategy Sharing	Strategy to figure out unfamiliar words: skip it; think of a word that would make sense; confirm your prediction using knowledge of letter-sound relationships.
Journal and Book Sharing	Illustrations support and extend meaning in books. Authors include biographical information for their audiences.
Quiet Reading Time	Children read a diverse range of materials to become familiar with various forms and functions of print. There is a relationship between written and spoken words when reading. Read print from the left to right and from the top to bottom of the page. Small words are often embedded in larger words. Sometimes readers make substitutions when words look alike, but they self-correct their reading if the words do not make sense.
Playground Stories	Children learn to represent ideas using art, mathematics, and language. Each communication system supports and extends the meaning potential of the others. Invented spelling reflects developing knowledge of letter-sound relationships.
Pen Pal Letters	Writing strategy: write what you want to say, not just what you can spell. A hyphen means the author divided the word. It is important to self-correct when you are reading if the words do not make sense. Spell words conventionally when you remember how they are constructed from reading and say words slowly to hear the sounds when you are writing unfamiliar words.

Supporting Readers. During the writing workshop, Vania read her newly published book to her teacher. When she came to the word *snake*, she looked to Tim for help. He reread the sentence, making the beginning sound of the word, and Vania immediately remembered that it said *snake*. In so doing, Tim devised a response that would help her predict using semantic and syntactic cues and confirm her prediction using graphophonemic cues. He wants his students to focus on meaning, and to do so he uses the strategy that he thinks will be most helpful for a particular child, given the context of the reading experience.

Reflecting on Writing Strategies. When Tony read his teacher the message for the class calendar, "I'm making a book," Tim asked him to share his thinking with the group. Tony explained his thinking by showing how he made a connection between the apostrophe in his teacher's last name (O'Keefe) and the word *I'm*. He also helped his teacher see that he uses visual memory to spell words he has seen in print. For example, Tony recalled *I'm* from his brother's book. He also said he knew that *I* has to be a capital letter and that all letters that follow are lower case. Finally, when asked about his spelling for *making*, which he spelled *macking*, Tony demonstrated his understanding that *ck* and *ing* go together. He simply overgeneralized the *ck* in this instance. He also stated that he figured out the beginning of the word, *ma*, by listening to the sounds. Tony's explanation highlighted how he used multiple strategies to construct and share meaning. He strategically accessed strategies that were most appropriate for different words and for different parts of words.

Editing for Publication. When Tim was helping Paul edit his book for publication, his strategy of using one letter to represent a word was validated as an effective way to convey meaning. The children discussed the fact that most of them probably employed this strategy when they were learning to write and that they usually chose the most dominant letters in the words to convey meaning.

Informal Strategy Sharing. As the children worked together during the writing workshop, they discussed a variety of strategies that could be used to help them figure out unfamiliar words. They came up with the following: "Skip it," "Think of a word that would make sense," and "Sound it out." Tim acknowledged each contribution, while he tried to help them see the importance of using all of the cue systems (graphophonemics, syntax, and semantics) in concert to construct meaning from print.

Journal and Book Sharing. The children emphasized the importance of sharing illustrations when reading published books to new audiences. They know the pictures convey meaning, too. Tim recognized the biographical sketch at the back of Vania's book, "Vania, girl, 6, Mr. O'Keefe," and discussed how professional authors include biographical information, like Vania did, when publishing books. This was just one example that illustrates how the teacher emphasizes the complementary processes of reading and writing while encouraging his learners to think like readers and writers.

Quiet Reading Time. The children were encouraged to read a diverse range of materials in order to develop sensitivity to the various forms and functions of print. They used a pointer when reading big books, thus focusing on the relationship between the written and spoken word and on the rhythm and flow of language. As the teacher listened to the children read, he informally monitored their strategies by reflecting on their miscues and analyzing them in relation to the cue systems being highlighted. Ray discovered that his name was embedded in the word *crayons*. Vania substituted the word *Zam*, her brother's name, for *Zans* in a Dr. Seuss book. She self-corrected her miscue, and her teacher indicated that he understood that she did so because the word *Zans* is graphophonemically similar to her brother's name. Her self-correction illustrated how readers in this class strive to construct meaning when reading.

Mathematics: Playground Stories. Tim created a popular class activity that was an extension of a survey that he conducted the previous day. He collaborated with Amanda to transform the survey data into a visual representation. They used art to "show" the choices made by the class. The decision to represent running by writing the child's name sideways, because "running goes sideways," and to represent walking by writing names vertically, because "walking goes up and down," represents the sophisticated problem-solving strategies that the children employed when moving from one sign system (writing) to another (art). When the children wrote their own playground stories using their friends' photos, they demonstrated their developing understanding of letter-sound relationships through their invented spellings. They also demonstrated their current conceptions of addition and subtraction when they used numbers to tell their stories. The fact that there are various ways to tell stories (such as art, writing, and equations) and each one has unique qualities was emphasized to help the children develop an appreciation for alternate forms of communication.

Pen Pal Letters. Tim used a book to introduce the pen pal letters because it highlighted the importance of "doing the best you can," revising, and "writing what you mean, not just what you can spell." The children had been engaged in authentic writing experiences with a real audience for several months, and the book simply solidified many of the insights about letter writing that the class had been exploring throughout the semester. Some of the children read their letters independently, while others used shared reading to give each other support. The children who were reading together helped each other by making recommendations ("Skip it like Kareem did"). Tim explained that one author used a hyphen to divide a word because she ran out of space. One child substituted the word *valentine* for *vacation* because *valentine* had been a popular word that spring, and because it was graphically similar in appearance to *vacation*. When Tony was reading the letter he had composed for his pen pal, he accidentally skipped a line. He immediately self-corrected "because it didn't make sense."

The children's writing strategies were also varied and reflected the children's current understanding of language. Michael often said words slowly when he was writing to capture the most evident sounds. Tony used this strategy when he came to new words, but he spelled common words fluently and conventionally using visual memory from reading. He used what he knew about language, particularly spelling patterns in English, to figure out unfamiliar words. Reconstructing his thinking made it clear that his decisions were logical, systematic, and rule-governed. A review of all of the letters produced this day reveals the fact that they were all unique in content and form.

A Final Note

This classroom sketch represents a typical day in April 1990. Just multiply the insights generated during that 7½-hour day by 180 days to understand the learning potential of this whole language classroom.

3 Tracing the Language Growth of Three Children

Kareem

"Mr. O'Keefe! I've uncovered something!" Kareem stood up and walked to the large chart paper on which Tim had written the poem "Could Be Halloween" (found in *Performable Poems*, compiled by P. P. Peek, Weekly Reader, 1981). The class had read the poem aloud several times, and it came to be one of their favorites. Stepping gingerly around his classmates, Kareem scanned the poem as he approached it. Finding the word *eyes*, he covered the first *e* with his right hand. "See *yes*? It's just the *e* that makes it *eyes*."

By showing the class, and the teacher, that the word *eyes* contained another smaller word within it and that the only difference between the two words was a single letter which totally changed not only the meaning of the word, but the sound as well, Kareem proved himself to be a strategic user of visual information. After thanking Kareem for sharing his discovery, Tim asked if anyone else noticed anything about the poem that they would like to share.

Thus began one of the most successful strategies used in the class that year. It became known simply as "What do you notice?" Words within words, punctuation, capitalization, unusual spellings, homonyms, rhyming words, and sound-symbol relationships were only a few of the myriad of observations made during group time. Kareem was always one of the first to volunteer this kind of information about print, and "What do you notice?" became known as "his" strategy.

Kareem had begun the school year like most of the students in this transition first-grade class. While Tim encouraged the children to write for meaning, Kareem's first journal entry was self-prescribed handwriting practice (see Figure 7). He began the first page of his journal with a row of *A*'s followed by two rows of *a*'s. Then he added a row of *B*'s, a row of *b*'s, a row of *K*'s, and finally his name.

Kareem had brought to school a working knowledge of letters and corresponding sounds, but he was reluctant to draw on it

Figure 7
Kareem's self-prescribed
writing practice,
1 September 1989.

when writing on his own. Much of his journal during the early part of the year was handwriting practice, writing the alphabet, and writing words he knew he could spell conventionally—including names of friends, classmates, and family members. Kareem also busied himself copying poems, color words, numerals, and words from a bulletin board containing environmental print. His journal seemed to be the most basic form of writing drill even though other children were writing stories and he was constantly asked to write meaningfully. Kareem adamantly retained ownership of his journal by using it for what seemed to Tim like manual labor.

However, in a written conversation with Tim on September 19th, Kareem demonstrated that he had some knowledge about sounds and symbols:

> *Where did you get that shirt?*
>
> Kame [K-Mart]
>
> *I really like it. Do you like Alf?*
>
> Yes
>
> *What else do you like?*
>
> Ktc [Cartoons]
>
> *Which cartoon do you like best?*
>
> Restooirmho [Roger Rabbit]

The word *K-Mart* was available on the bulletin board of

environmental print. Kareem chose to write it his own way, *Kame*, indicating a willingness to take risks with spelling when recording his meaning. Kareem picked up the initial *k* and long *a*. He also included the *m* he heard in the word. In response to the question about Alf, Kareem used the conventional spelling of *yes*, but he was not satisfied with his own penmanship. After erasing his first attempt (also spelled conventionally), he improved his handwriting on the second try. The way Kareem wrote the word *cartoons*, spelled *Ktc*, clearly demonstrates how much attention he paid to the letter sounds in written language. While his spelling was not standard, he picked out three of the more prominent consonant letter sounds and wrote them down in the order that he heard them when saying the word to himself. His version of *Roger Rabbit*, spelled *Restooirmho*, does not correspond as closely to the conventional spelling, yet Tim was delighted that he took a risk.

Later in the fall, Tim noticed that Kareem was beginning to use the strategy of writing and then reading to help him spell a word conventionally. For example, one morning during writing workshop, Tim was writing messages to the children in the room. Tim asked Kareem to help spell *Chiquita*, the name of one of the children in the class. Kareem responded, "I can't spell it, but I *can* write it." With that he took a piece of scrap paper and wrote the name. Not satisfied with the first trial, he wrote her name a second time, this time spelling it correctly. At the next class meeting, Kareem shared his strategy. Standing at the front of the group, he used the example with Chiquita's name to show how he wrote the word twice in order to figure out which one looked right.

Tim validated this visual memory strategy by commenting, "Sometimes I have problems spelling words too. Often I'll do what Kareem did. Write the word the best I can, then read it to see if it looks right to me." In this way, Tim legitimized Kareem's strategy publicly and reinforced its use by Kareem and the rest of the class.

By the end of October, Kareem started to break away from his "safe" journal writing projects and ventured into writing stories. Kareem wrote the following story (see Figure 8) on October 25th: "Once there was a mouse who wanted something to eat. He found it. Something. He ate it. The cheese. Found his mama. The end." This journal entry clearly shows Kareem's use of letter-sound relationships and the growing number of words that he could spell conventionally. It is important to notice in this writing sample that Kareem changed from writing as merely an exercise to writing to record his thoughts. His use of letter sounds supports the process of making his ideas more permanent by writing them down. Quickly writing in green crayon, Kareem ignored the lines on the

Figure 8
Kareem's journal entry for
25 October 1989.

Figure 9
Kareem's journal entry for
16 November 1989.

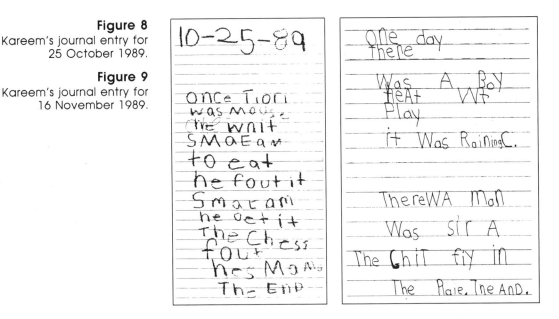

page in his notebook and focused most of his attention on the content of his story.

Kareem's journal entry dated November 16th (see Figure 9) indicates a growing concern with his reader. Using a black pen, Kareem wrote the following story on the lines of his notebook: "One day there was a boy that wanted to play. It was raining." Then he wrote a second story: "There was a man who saw a ghost fly in the air. The end." Kareem separated his stories with three blank lines, left spaces between words, and attended closely to grapheme-phoneme relationships. After writing these pieces, Kareem proudly asked Tim to read them. He realized that his attention to handwriting, spacing, and letter sounds was closely associated with the ability of another person to read his text, unaided. He was learning that the more attention the writer pays to spelling and other conventions, the easier it is for someone to understand the intended message.

Late that month, Kareem created a number story in which one unfortunate creature was to be subtracted by getting eaten. Kareem selected a shark and a whale to do the deed and glued them on top of a penguin so that only its feet and printed name were left showing. With a red crayon, Kareem drew the blood around the attackers. He wrote the following: "There was a penguin and he got eaten." Kareem represented his story numerically by $1 - 1 = 0$. Kareem's sophisticated use of sound-symbol relationships reflected his growth and his concern for his readers. By

Figure 10
Kareem's journal entry for early 1990.

Figure 11
Kareem's journal entry for 22 February 1990.

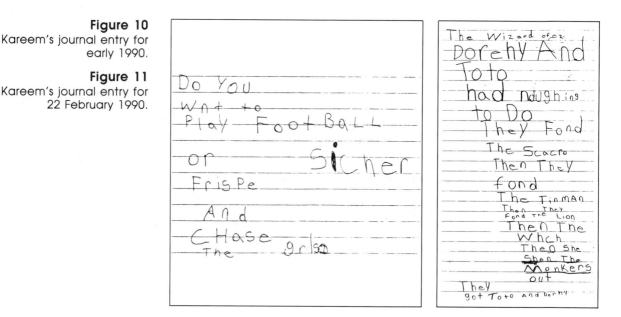

this time, late November, Tim and others in the class could read, unaided, most of Kareem's writing. Kareem substituted the word *in* for *and* in this story, but this was logical in that it corresponded closely to his pronunciation of the word.

Kareem began to enjoy "messing around" with language in his journal. On one occasion he connected food words that "go together" with arrows, writing "pcan → pie" and "app → pie." Another day, in late January, Kareem turned words into a game by playing "Hangman" with a classmate using the words *rabbit* and *free*. In the same journal entry, Kareem experimented with a "fancy way" to write by adding serifs to his letters. This behavior is similar to the way in which young children play around with oral language when learning to talk.

By February, Kareem's personal journal had become a functional document for recording thoughts, current events, and drafts of stories, many of which became books that he published and contributed to the class library. One day Kareem used his journal to create a set of options for himself and his friends about what they could do for recess (see Figure 10). "Do you want to play football," wrote Kareem, "soccer, or frisbee and chase the girls?"

Later, on February 22nd, Kareem used his journal to record the following summary of the current chapter book that Tim was reading to the class, *The Wizard of Oz* by L. Frank Baum (Doubleday, 1900, 1944): "Dorothy and Toto had nothing to do. They found the Scarecrow. Then they found the Tinman. Then they found the Lion. Then the witch. Then she sent the monkeys out. They got Toto and Dorothy." By this point Kareem had internalized an understanding of graphophonemic relationships and used them easily and naturally, even though he was communicating to no one but himself (see Figure 11).

As the year progressed, Kareem's knowledge about sound-symbol relationships continued to develop. One day in early March, Kareem and two of his classmates, Vania and Stephen, were busy writing words on the board. When it was time for Kareem to work with Tim, Kareem circled the following columns of words on the board and explained that he wanted to save these and share them with the rest of the class:

he	and	who	he
fall	an	bears	see
all	hen	fears	we
	pen	pears	me
	cen	sears	
	fen	zoo	
		zooms	
		tooms	
		fooms	

The children had started by writing down words they knew; then they changed or added letters to create new words, exploring consistencies and inconsistencies in letter patterns and in sound-symbol relationships. When reading the list, the children noted which words were simply "made-up words" so that the class would realize they knew the difference. As Kareem read the third column of words for the class, "who, bears, fears [pronounced *fairs*], pears, sears," he interrupted himself: "I know that one. It's like the store, but it doesn't sound like these others." Kareem and the others in this self-initiated study group taught the class another lesson about letter-sound relationships—drawing particular attention to the fact that there are exceptions to phonics generalizations. Kareem and his comrades showed that most words which end the same rhyme, but, at the same time, many words that end similarly do not *necessarily* have the same sounds. In this presentation, the three children demonstrated both a simple rule pattern and an exception to that rule.

In January, the class started dialogue journals in which Tim and Sandra Pees, the class tutor, would correspond with the children once or twice each week. Tim saw these journals as a good

Figure 12
Kareem's dialogue journal,
20 March 1990.

How did you do on the test?

fine

DiD You went
to The Bech

No, I stayed home.

what is your phone number?

796 - 23 - 47

Whre is Your
MoTher?

She is in Mexico.

way to evaluate the children's progress and to demonstrate writing conventions in a context where the focus was on meaning. In one of these dialogues with Tim in March, Kareem noticed a spelling anomaly (see Figure 12). When Tim wrote to Kareem, "What is your phone number?" Kareem responded verbally, "*That's* how you spell *phone?* I thought it started with an *f!*"

"I can see why you thought that," replied Tim. "It does sound like an *f.*"

"I know now," Kareem came back, "it's like *telephone* and *elephant*. The *ph* sounds like an *f.*" When Kareem shared this discovery about *ph* and how he made the connection between its use in this context and with other words, he provided another lesson to the class on letter sounds; some sounds are represented by several letter pattern combinations while some letters make multiple sounds depending on adjoining letters in words.

As the year progressed and Kareem overcame his concern for skills and rehearsing old knowledge, he began writing connected texts for a variety of purposes. In so doing, he grew in his understanding and use of letter sounds and used them in concert with other cue systems to convey meaningful messages. The more Kareem made use of his knowledge of sound-symbol relationships, by generating hypotheses and testing them, the more he learned about these relationships.

Like many of his classmates, Kareem enjoyed the "Teenage Mutant Ninja Turtles" television show and toys. The Turtles fre-

Figure 13
Kareem's journal entry for
19 May 1990.

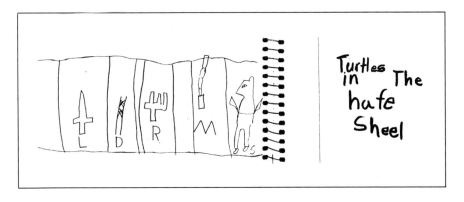

quently showed up in his journal and independent writing projects. In one journal entry dated May 19th (see Figure 13), Kareem
represented each of five main characters by drawing the weapon
associated with each character and writing the first letter of the
corresponding character's name underneath. On the facing journal
page he wrote, "Turtles in the hafe sheel." In an earlier journal
entry, that of April 2nd, Kareem came quite close to the conventional spelling of his favorite character in the group, Michaelangelo, writing *Michalandglow.*

While it is clear that Kareem used letter sounds to pull the
spelling together, he also employed some different strategies as
well. One of his classmates was named Michael, and on April
24th, Kareem incorporated Michael's name when he wrote Michaelangelo's name, writing *Michaelandjelo.* In both versions, Kareem used
the word *and* for the third syllable of Michaelangelo's name, a
word Kareem knew how to spell. For the fourth and fifth syllables
Kareem depended on his current knowledge of sound-symbol relationships. Both attempts indicate a high level of success. He wrote
the words using his current knowledge about language, and, most
importantly, both versions of the name effectively conveyed the
meaning that Kareem wanted to record.

Kareem was always fascinated by the anomalies that he encountered, and he often brought them to the attention of his
teachers and classmates. At the end of May, Kareem was reading a
version of *The Three Billy Goats Gruff* retold by Mae Knight Pallium
(Macmillan, 1967). Approaching Tim with book in hand, Kareem
declared, "Mr. O'Keefe, I saw Knight Rider on TV, and they spell
night with a *k.* It must be a silent *k.* Look, it's just like this book."

A week later, on a class field trip to a nearby park, Kareem
was talking to his teacher when he saw a truck drive by. "Look
Mr. O'Keefe! That truck says 'OVERNITE.' That *night* is different
from the other ones, *night* like 'night time' and 'Knight Rider.'"

Kareem's curious nature and his determination to seek out patterns and exceptions allowed him to use graphophonemics as one powerful tool to read and write meaningfully.

Jessica   About one week before the end of school, Tim asked several children to go through their writing files and to find a piece of writing from earlier in the school year that they could compare with a more recent piece. Jessica selected a story she had written on September 27th to compare with her latest picture story of May 28th. The first was a picture of five puppies racing toward a bowl of dog food, with the following story: "The dogs was racing to the food. They love that food. They so little. They like that sky. They like me." Jessica's more recent story (see Figure 14), based on a picture of two sunbathers, contained the following text: "The man and the woman was laying down to get a suntan and they was at the beach! They in their chairs. The clouds was white. They had the bathing suits on! They have their eyes closed!"
Tim asked Jessica to look at both samples and to think about how she had changed as a writer over the school year. She responded:

> I think it's changed because I left spaces on the new one but not
> on the old one. Also, I didn't put any exclamation points or pe-
> riods on the old one. I writed my c's backwards and I putted my h
> in upper case. It should have been a little one. I'm a better speller
> now. *Much* better than I did then. I also writed more [on the recent
> entry], and it didn't take me so much time. Now I'm using letters
> to help me figure out stuff, you know, how to spell and write.

Jessica's analysis of her writing ability was amazing in its depth. She accounted for improvements in her handwriting (properly written letters, spaces between words), punctuation (periods and exclamation points), capitalization, the amount that she wrote, and how fluent she had become as a writer (the fact that it took less time to write more in the second piece). While Tim appreciated Jessica's attention to how she changed in her use of conventions, it was also apparent to him that the content of Jessica's writing had also matured. While neither piece was truly a story, the sample from May shows more attention to description.
In her analysis, what seemed to catch Jessica's attention more than anything else was her growing use of letters and words to help her record her thoughts. She noticed that her spelling was "*much* better" than it used to be and that she was using letters to help "figure out stuff, you know, how to spell and write." In a classroom where graphophonemics was taught only in connection

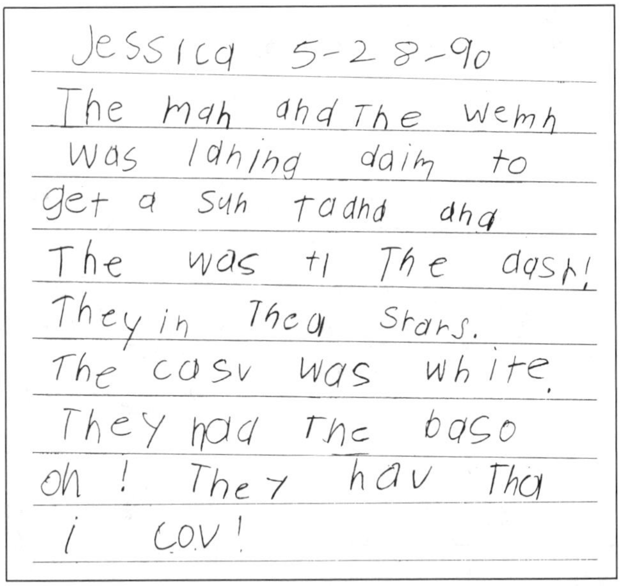

Figure 14
Jessica's journal entry for
28 May 1990.

Jessica 5-28-90
The man and The wemn
was lahing daim to
get a suh tadnd dnd
The was tl The dash!
They in They Stars.
The casv was white.
They had The baso
oh! They hav Tha
i cov!

with making meaning, Jessica shows that it was an important cue system for her, one that she could use, in concert with other cue systems, to help her make meaning. During her year in the transition first-grade class, Jessica went from using letters in a seemingly random fashion to using letters associated with their corresponding sounds, a very important step for Jessica in her journey toward authorship.

While Jessica did not make as much progress as Kareem, her growth in one year was nonetheless impressive. Many of her early journal entries were drawings; print played a very small role for her. Indeed, it often seemed that had Tim not asked the children to write something each day in their notebooks, Jessica would not have written at all. Sometimes she merely wrote her name on the page. Other days she would write from her "safe" words or words in the environment—including copying the names of her friends from the large, alphabetized chart kept in the front of the room. This was not unlike many children in the class who thought that writing for them meant getting something down on paper that grown-ups would consider correct. At six years of age, they had already brought with them an instructional history of what was "right" and "wrong."

Tim worked to help Jessica overcome her concern for correctness. The following portion of a written conversation with Tim on September 20th (see Figure 15) shows how effectively Jessica took risks with print in her writing:

Figure 15
Jessica's dialogue journal,
20 September 1989.

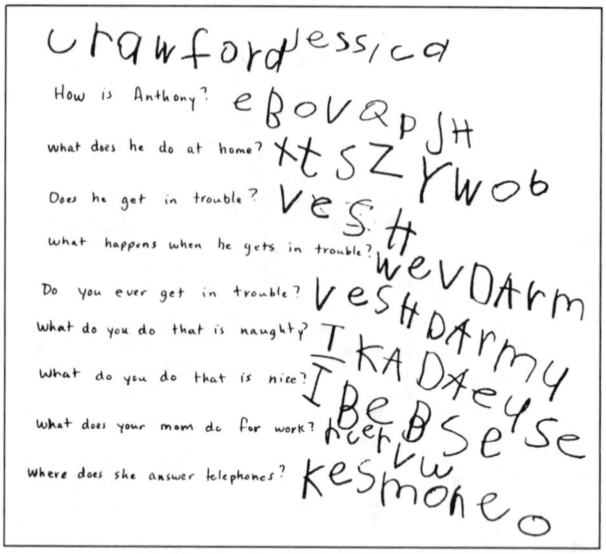

How is Anthony?

He is fine.

What does he do at home?

He skates in the house.

Does he get in trouble?

Yes.

What happens when he gets in trouble?

Mama hollers at him.

Do you ever get in trouble?

Yes, I do. When I'm naughty.

What do you do that is naughty?

I take his toys.

What do you do that is nice?

I buy him something this morning.

Her answers to Tim's questions were logical, and while she did not yet make use of letter-sound relationships in writing down letters, she unself-consciously recorded her answers and assigned meaning to her writing by reading her answers aloud as she wrote. She knew that in writing *ebovqpjh* she was expressing the thought "He is fine." Constant encouragement and acceptance of all drafts allowed Jessica to write down her ideas successfully regardless of her experience with letter-sound relationships.

Figure 16
Jessica's journal entry for
25 September 1989.

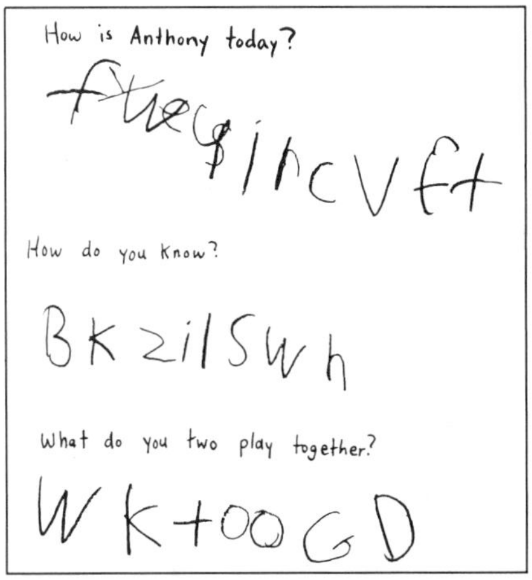

Figure 17
Jessica's journal entry for
6 October 1989.

A few days later, on September 25th, Jessica's journal entry covered two pages. The first page contained color words copied from color collages that the class had made and displayed on the side wall above the children's cubbies. With each color word, Jessica wrote with the appropriate color, using the markers and crayons in front of her. On her next page (see Figure 16), she made a swirling drawing similar to diagrams the children had seen in newspapers and on television tracking the path of Hurricane Hugo as it approached their state. Underneath her drawing, Jessica wrote "in cursive" with a red marker. Her tight, linear writing crossed two lines of her notebook. After each line, she went back and put some dots over her writing, apparently accessing cursive writing demonstrations she had witnessed sometime earlier. Jessica then drew three rectangular shapes caught up in her spiral drawing and signed her name at the top of the page. When asked to read what she had written, Jessica, again reflecting intentionality, answered, "The cars are flying up in the hurricane."

Jessica's writing on this day shows her willingness to take risks with print in a nonthreatening situation, such as journal writing. She playfully used what she called "curfis" (cursive) to represent her spoken words. Her linear scribbles do resemble cursive writing and performed its function: giving meaning.

The next day Jessica abandoned her cursive writing to record hurricane events in her notebook. She announced that she had written "My friend's house. A tree fell down." Her artwork clearly corresponded to her written text. Because Jessica felt free to write her ideas and have her messages valued for their meaning, she was very comfortable experimenting with print. While she was not yet using letter-sound relationships in her own writing, she was

Figure 18
Jessica's journal entry for
9 October 1989.

able to connect letter sounds with letters when helping friends write or when suggesting spellings for language experience stories cooperatively written by the class and recorded by Tim.

By the beginning of October, Jessica started to use graphophonemics in her own writing projects. In a written conversation from October 6th, for example, Jessica displayed her willingness to attempt spelling using her knowledge of letters and their corresponding sounds in print (see Figure 17). When Tim asked Jessica to read her first answer, she responded "Fine." Tim repeated her answer, stressing the initial *f* sound. "Just a minute," said Jessica, and she erased her first response (*nyes*) and rewrote her answer to start with an *f*, *fwyircvft*.

To answer the second question in their written conversation, Jessica told Tim what she wanted to say, "Because I live with him," and then asked him to say the words back to her, slowly. This time she recorded a more graphophonemically connected choice of letters for her answer, *bkzilswh*. Jessica effectively picked out three consonant sounds for the word *because* (*bkz*) and wrote *i* for *I*, *ls* for *live*, and the initial consonant for *with* (*w*) and *him* (*h*). By asking Tim to repeat her own words to her slowly, Jessica was strategically demonstrating the need for assistance with letter-sound relationships. She was showing Tim how to help her.

In response to the question inquiring about what the two children played together, Jessica relied less on Tim and discovered she could manage on her own by saying the words slowly to herself, thus writing "We color together" as *wktoogd*. While Jessica mainly picked out consonant sounds to represent, she also complemented her new sounding-out strategy with a word she knew. Jessica began writing the word *together* by using a word which she

Figure 19
Jessica's journal entry for
14 October 1989.

Figure 20
Jessica's journal entry for
8 November 1989.

knew and which sounded like it fit—*too*. While she was gently nudged by her teacher, who knew her well enough to know that she was ready to begin exploring letter-sound patterns, Jessica took charge of this mini "lesson" by attending to Tim's demonstrations and building on her current understandings.

Three days later, on October 9th, Jessica showed that she could use letters and sounds together on her own, without an adult close by to help her (see Figure 18). When writing about the current chapter book Tim was reading to the class, *Charlotte's Web* by E. B. White (Harper and Row, 1952), Jessica illustrated that she was doing more than writing letters randomly, which she had done only a week earlier. Her series of letters, *thepsvbyvemvsdtso*, represented what she wanted to say, "The pig saw his best friend and it was a spider." While there is not a one-to-one relationship between the graphophonemic relationships in the words and Jessica's written representation of them, it is apparent that Jessica did draw on her current knowledge of this cue system in this sample.

With Jessica, as with many children, her writing growth was not an entirely linear process. Like many others, Jessica went back and forth, sometimes putting effort into matching letters with sounds and sometimes directing her attention to other aspects of her language projects. About one week later during another writing project involving *Charlotte's Web*, Jessica went back to writing letters to express her meaning with much less consideration of their corresponding sounds (see Figure 19). Her intended meaning ("They were sleeping in the night. Charlotte found a bug in her web") cannot be determined from her writing.

During the second week in November, Jessica recorded in her journal a picture with corresponding text which nicely illustrates her movement again, which included the use of corresponding letters and sounds in her independent writing (see Figure 20). Here her intended meaning was quite clear: "Once upon a time

Figure 21
Jessica's journal entry for
10 January 1990.

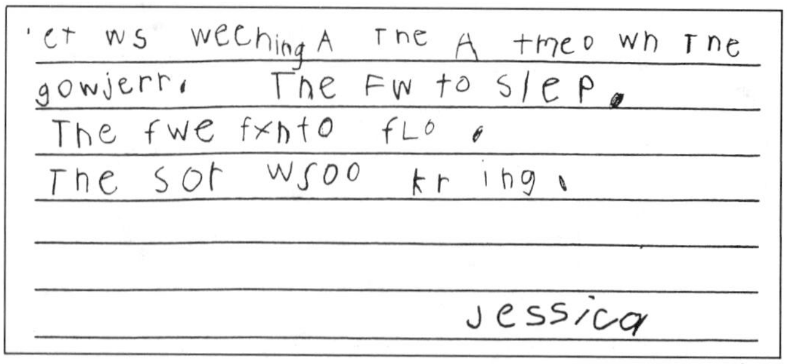

'ct ws weching A Tne A tmeo wh Tne
gowjerr. The Fw to slep.
The fwe fxhto fLo
The sor wʃoo kr ihg

                                    Jessica

there was a spider in the box swinging." In this sample, Jessica also left large spaces between her words, a convention which she adopted and abandoned several times over the next few months, again showing that writing growth is not a linear, sequential process.

By January, Jessica was continuing to refine her use of letters corresponding to sounds and began to add other conventions. While punctuation was continually discussed in class in the context of written language, it was not until after the winter break that Jessica used it in her writing regularly. A picture story from January 10th illustrates the ease with which Jessica wrote her description (see Figure 21). The text of her story read as follows: "It was raining and the animals went in the garage. The fox went to sleep. The fence was fixin' to fall. The squirrel was crying."

In this sample, Jessica added some letters along with the letter sounds that she could hear when saying the words slowly to herself (*gowjerr* for *garage*, *wsoo* for *was*). Tim thought that she was perhaps extending the length of her words to match more closely the length of the words that she had seen in print. Many of Jessica's invented spellings were similar to those used by her colleagues. For instance, *it* was commonly spelled *et*. The logic of this choice is apparent when considering that children wrote words the way they pronounced them. This indicates a concern for matching the way a word is written with the way it sounds.

After listening to L. Frank Baum's classic, *The Wizard of Oz*, the children watched a part of the film for each of three days. Following each movie segment, they wrote about the story in their journals. In a journal entry for January 17th (see Figure 22), Jessica chose to write about something that was in the movie, but not in the book: "Dorothy when she was sitting beside the chair. She saw her Aunt Em in the bubble."

By this time, Jessica was writing quickly and freely and rarely asked for assistance when spelling new words. Invented spelling had become a tool on which she came to rely to make her

Figure 22
Jessica's journal entry for
17 January 1990.

Figure 23
Jessica's dialogue journal,
30 April 1990.

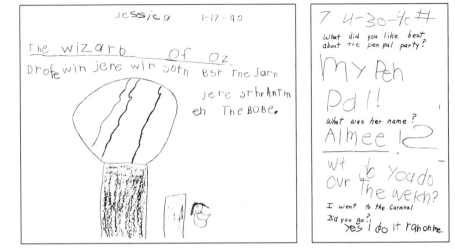

writing clear, concise, and readable by others. It helped her make her thoughts permanent and left no doubt about what she was thinking at the time she wrote. While she had not isolated every letter sound, it is clear that she was becoming more logical and systematic in her choices of letters to represent the sounds in the words as she said them to herself.

In an April entry in Jessica's dialogue journal (see Figure 23), she responded to Sandra's questions about the recent get-together of the transition first-grade class with an undergraduate class of Elementary Education Language Arts Methods students who had been pen pals with the children for several months. In this short, written question-and-answer period, Jessica showed that she was quite precocious with writing. She answered Sandra's first question and used an exclamation point for emphasis—as if to say, "Silly question!" Sandra's second question made Jessica recall an unusual spelling of her pen pal's first name, Aimee, but since Jessica had used it several times in the context of letter writing, she spelled it correctly. Next, Jessica wrote a question asking about Sandra's weekend. When Sandra turned the question about going to the carnival back to Jessica, she went beyond the obligatory one-word answer and described the conditions of the carnival visit as well ("Yes, I did. It rained on me."). By this time not only was Jessica writing to communicate, which she could do early in the year, but she had gained enough experience with written language to have her writing read by others with little or no assistance.

By looking at samples of Jessica's writing over time, it is clear that she used graphophonemics through invented spelling as an important tool in her written communication. While her growth was not linear, she felt trusted enough as a learner to experiment and test hypotheses about writing. Although considered by the district to be an "at-risk" student, as were all of the transition first graders, Jessica became a competent user of written language.

At the beginning of the school year and then again at the end of May, the children were asked to draw pictures of themselves and to write something to accompany their pictures. By comparing these two samples of young Jessica's talent (see Figures 24 and 25), it is easy to see how far she had come as a writer. Her writing in the first self-portrait needed to be deciphered ("I like myself. I love my mom."), but her comments in the second self-portrait are easily understood: "I am 7 and I am pretty! My friend is spending the night. We made a plant! I jump a lot!"

Tony

In April, Tony was asked to reflect on how he had changed as a writer. Using his journal, he looked at specific pieces of his writing over time and made some interesting comments and observations about the processes involved in his becoming a better writer. Through his reflections, he also showed insights into his reading and writing strategies.

"Well, when I was at the beginning of the year, I didn't even know how to spell *cat*," Tony began. "I spelled it the best way I could." Looking at an example of *cats* spelled correctly, Tony commented on how he eventually figured it out. "Because *a*, if it's with another vowel, it says its own name. If there's a vowel at the very back or if two vowels are together. But I just took one vowel to have it say *cats*."

In Tony's classroom instruction, phonics rules had been taught only in the context of natural language events. Tony had drawn from these experiences to explain the spelling of a simple, one-syllable word. Whether or not he really used this rather complicated procedure to uncover the spelling is secondary to the fact that he realized that generalizations about sound-symbol relationships did exist.

Tony continued: "I did not know how to spell *lion* until we went to the zoo, and I heard the word and I read it for the first time. I kept putting *s*'s, and then I remembered that was just for lots of them. So I finally erased the *s* and that's how I learned how to spell *lion*."

When Tony was asked how he figured out how to write new words that he did not remember seeing previously, he replied, "If I don't remember seeing it, I try to find it."

"What if you want a word and you can't find it and it's important for your story?" Tony was asked.

Figure 24
Jessica's first self-portrait,
August 1989.

Figure 25
Jessica's final self-portrait,
25 May 1990.

"I would try to ask someone," Tony said. "Or sound it out."

Tony was an excellent risk taker in his writing. Most of the time he wrote in invented spelling. Over the year, he also became adept at using words he had encountered earlier as a reader.

In the April interview, Tony was looking at a book of his published earlier in the year and a more recent one (see Figures 26 and 27). "See, this is where I messed up. Look!" emphasized Tony, referring to the cover of his earlier book. "You can tell the difference, *by*." On the earlier book Tony had spelled the word *biy*. By the time he wrote the later book, he knew the correct spelling was *by*.

"You used to spell it *biy*, and now you spell it *by*. Why did you put the *i* in the first one?" Tony was asked.

"I thought it said *buh-eye*." Tony answered, enunciating the letter sounds he heard. "I just heard the *i*."

These types of comments suggest that Tony was not a passive recipient of abstract rules, but rather that he was active in creating his own insights into the regularities and patterns in the English language. It was largely because Tony was encouraged to take risks and to record his ideas in his own way that he could eventually step back and think about the consistencies and inconsistencies in written language.

Tony began the year like most children in the class. He had to be coaxed into writing because of his belief that he could not write. This is a position taken by most of the children entering Tim's transition first-grade class. One of Tim's first responsibilities was to show the children that they could indeed convey meaning with print. "Just write it the best you can" became a standard

Figure 26
Tony's book prepared early
in the school year.

Figure 27
Tony's book prepared near
the end of the school year.

reply. When it became apparent that Tim was going to accept all of the children's drafts, they gradually let go of the idea that they could not write.

Tony's first self-portrait with a writing sample showed little obvious letter-sound connection (see Figure 28). His text read: "I went to play outside. I helped my Mommy bake cookies." However, this project and others which required the children simply to write what they wanted to say—the best they could—were important steps in getting the students to be confident risk takers. The focus was clearly on *what* they wanted to record and not *how,* for Tim believes that children learn the connections of language by using language to communicate and to learn.

On October 16th, during the reading of the class's first chapter book, *Charlotte's Web,* Tony drew a picture and wrote about a section of the story he remembered (see Figure 29): "Templeton eat food in the trough. [Charlotte said] Calm down, Wilbur." When Tony read his writing aloud, Tim noticed for the first time that Tony was making a clear and conscious connection between the words he had written and the ones he spoke when reading. Tony spoke his words slowly and carefully and extracted the letter sounds which he had recorded in his written text.

Tony's writing was shared with the rest of the class. His own invented spelling was recorded on the chalkboard so that the rest of the class could observe and benefit from Tony's writing. This not only reinforced Tony's strategies, but it also let Tony's peers in on the idea of using letters and sounds together when writing and reading. Additionally, the rest of the children were able to see one

Figure 28
Tony's first self-portrait,
August 1989.

Figure 29
Tony's journal entry for
16 October 1989.

of themselves in the role of teacher. Peer teaching was an important aspect of the curriculum which Tony helped to convey to his classmates.

Two days later, in a written conversation with his teacher about *Charlotte's Web,* Tony again proved that he was fast becoming adept at putting letter sounds together with words that he knew and that he could find in the environment in order to make his written text understandable to others (see Figure 30). Graphophonemics became another cue to assist Tony in the process of conveying meaning. His responses to Tim's questions were generally readable:

> *Did you like the book or the movie better?*
>
> The book.
>
> *Why did you like the book better?*
>
> Because the Uncle.
>
> *Uncle was in both.*
>
> Why do you like Templeton?
>
> *I liked him because he was sneaky. Do you think he was sneaky?*
>
> Yes, I do.

In this dialogue, Tony left spaces between his words in his first two responses. For his question, he properly used a question mark, which was somewhat surprising since prior to this he had shown no interest in using punctuation—not even periods—in his own writing. Perhaps the natural demonstrations provided in written conversation were all that he needed to prompt him to attend

Figure 30
Tony's journal entry for
18 October 1989.

to punctuation in this context. Throughout this text, Tony's use of letter sounds is obvious. He was comfortable simply spelling his best for unknown words, and he took the strategic approach of looking in the book for the spelling of *Templeton* and *Charlotte's Web*. His answers and question were logical and well thought-out. When he was asked, "Why did you like the book better?" Tony answered, "Because the Uncle." Tim then responded that "Uncle" was in both the book and the video, to which Tony answered verbally, "I know, but I like the picture better in the book."

While this dialogue shows that much of Tony's spelling was far from standard, his choice of letters to represent the sounds was logical and showed a marked improvement from a couple of weeks earlier, when he was writing letters nearly at random to represent his meaning. Tony demonstrated that form does develop through functional use.

In a math story written in late November (see Figure 31), Tony showed that he was continuing to develop as a writer. He completely stopped writing random letters in favor of systematic invented spelling and words that he could spell conventionally. The story involved pictures of eight animals. Tony colored bright red spots for blood on the walrus and snake at the bottom of his page to indicate the dead characters and drew a tree to harbor the cowards, who were safely away from danger. Tony's artwork and text, including his equation, succinctly portrayed the action in his story: "Two animals died. And two are cowards. $8 - 2 = 6$." His

Figure 31
Tony's math story,
28 November 1989.

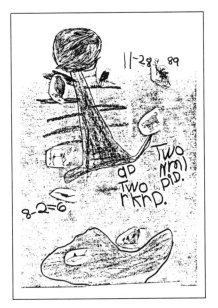

two sentences showed his consistent use of grapheme-phoneme relationships and included the number word *two*, which he had committed to memory by using it meaningfully in other contexts.

On December 13th, Tony wrote several messages he intended to read to the class at the next class meeting (see Figure 32):

> I like my family.
>
> I like Mr. O'Keefe and Mrs. Pees.
>
> I like Mr. Bear. He plays with me. I like school.
>
> I am going to Walt Disney World.

By using familiar words that he could spell (*I, like, going, to, Mr., he, me, Mr. O'Keefe, Mrs. Pees*) and by mixing these in with spellings he invented and with words he could find in the classroom environment, Tony proved that he could go beyond merely sounding out words to create his texts. He was using multiple skills and strategies to write, and while graphophonemics was obviously an important cue system, it was used only in concert with others to record the thoughts that he wanted to share with the class.

During the first semester, Tony's journal-writing time was mainly taken up with artwork and lists, which included friends, days of the week, colors, initials of his peers, number words, animal words, and words from the environmental print bulletin board. Beginning in February, a wonderful change took place in

Figure 32
Tony's journal entry for
13 December 1989.

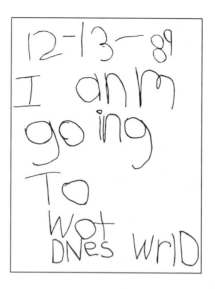

Tony and many others in the class. Vania, a classmate of Tony's,
wrote a story in her journal over the course of several days. When
she was finished, Tim asked if she would like to edit the story and
publish it as a book for the class library. Her enthusiastic effort
yielded a book called "A Cat and a Dog," to which the class
responded very positively.

While story writing was always an option during journal
time, Tim made it a point to emphasize the invitation to write
drafts and publish stories. Tony accepted the invitation eagerly and
began to use his journal time almost exclusively to create drafts of
stories which he would take to informal author circles, read aloud
to the class, and publish for the class library. While Vania's original
story was about four pages long, Tony's "The Squirrel and the
Rabbit" was twenty-eight pages from start to finish. He enlisted
the aid of two classmates on the rewrite and illustrations and listed
them and his teacher as coauthors. Tony spent almost three weeks
on the writing and editing of the rough draft and another week
rewriting and illustrating his book. After he had worked on the
story for several days, the story itself became the important thing
for Tony, and the actual publishing became secondary. The class
and Tim were in awe of Tony's persistence, and he gave progress
reports almost daily as to where he was in his story. Tony never
wanted to go more than a couple of days without reading his
entire work-in-progress to his teacher or his peers. There was
much more to Tony's story than the actual words on the page;
Tony made little asides to explain the action and used a great deal
of emphasis and many gestures when reading his story aloud.

Figure 33
Tony's journal entry for
18 April 1990.

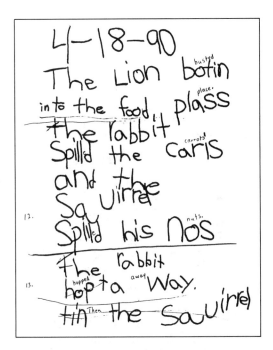

Tony did most of his editing as he worked on the story. Every day after reading the text to catch up to where he was in his story and then writing for ten to fifteen minutes, he would read his newest installment to Tim or Sandra and to a group of interested friends. It was at this point that questions about the story line and conventions of print would be raised and answered. Tony often erased and made changes on the spot or would ask the teacher to "write it the grown-up way" in the side column next to his text. Other times Tim would assist by writing conventionally spelled words over Tony's words or add omitted letters and words into Tony's text (see Figure 33).

One day, after getting a little frustrated while working on his story, Tony asked Tim to write for him as he dictated the ending of the story. Tim was happy to oblige. Tony's completed text was twenty-eight pages long and contained twenty-two illustrations (see Figures 34 and 35 for two sample pages). The full text read as follows:

> One day a little squirrel came out. He did not have a mom and he left the hole. He met a rabbit and he played with the rabbit. A lion jumped on the rabbit! The squirrel jumped and scratched the lion. The lion looked at the squirrel. And the lion let the rabbit go. The rabbit said to the squirrel, "Do you want any carrots?" "Nah, I will get nuts." So they went to get nuts and carrots. The lion

Figure 34
Sample page from
Tony's book.

Figure 35
Sample page from
Tony's book.

busted into the food place! The rabbit spilled the carrots and the squirrel spilled the nuts. The rabbit hopped away. Then the squirrel lost the rabbit. He was sad. He said, "I wish that I had those nuts." Then he met the lion. The lion tried to kill the squirrel. But the lion died. The squirrel and the rabbit jumped on him. A gorilla came right in front of the rabbit and the squirrel! He swung off of the big cliff! He tried to kill the rabbit! The gorilla swung and caught the rabbit! When the gorilla got back on the cliff the squirrel jumped on the gorilla and knocked him off. The gorilla died. The squirrel jumped on one of the branches. There was another squirrel's house. The rabbit hopped over on the tree. They went back to get something else to eat. They lived happily ever after. The End.

In writing "The Squirrel and the Rabbit," Tony thought like an author. He wrote, read, wrote again, drew from previous experiences with stories, conferred with his colleagues and mentors, self-corrected, edited, rewrote, illustrated, and contracted the services of others to help with the illustrations. He had ownership of his text, chose the cover, and did the general layout of the book himself. Tony also grew in his understanding and use of conventions. As he orchestrated the editing process, he learned the standard spelling for many new words. For example, after seeing *squirrel* spelled conventionally after his first author's circle, he switched from *skaeeal* to *squirrel* and continued to spell it correctly for the rest of his draft. In addition, Tony learned to use quotation marks and subsequently used them several times in other writing projects.

However, when Tony was writing his draft, he wrote out his text "the best he could." The conventions of print became secondary to the story itself. His concern for spelling, punctuation, and capitalization came after the creative, story-writing process each day—just as it should have. If Tony's story had been governed by the words he could spell correctly, or if his main concern had been for the rules of written language, it would not have been much of a story. Because he felt free to write meaningfully and to spell in his own way, Tony was free to create the story line he wanted. Tony's perseverance and his connectedness to his story and characters made him an excellent role model for his peers. Through the process of writing "The Squirrel and the Rabbit," Tony not only refined his ability to use sound-symbol relationships, but he did it in a way which served a much larger purpose, the recording of meaning.

Teaching in Support of Learning

As we explored *how* and *what* children learned in this whole language classroom, we found it helpful to take different cuts in our data. Each slice provided a unique perspective from which we could look. Chapter 2 highlighted the richness and complexity of the curriculum by portraying a typical day. The case studies in chapter 3, while emphasizing the role of graphophonemics in Tim's classroom, gave a different perspective. Traveling across a nine-month period enabled us to take a close look at three different children and at the similarities and differences in how they constructed knowledge about sound-symbol relationships. Here in chapter 4 we explore the teaching strategies that seemed to make a difference in this context. A general description of specific teaching strategies and corresponding classroom vignettes follow. We hope that this chapter will make Tim's role in this whole language classroom more visible.

Teaching Strategies Used in Tim's Classroom

What Do You Notice?

Songs, poems, and fingerplays are an integral part of the curriculum. Tim believes that they play an important role in helping children make connections between oral and written language. He frequently writes the words to the text on a large piece of chart paper, encouraging the children to watch as he writes so that he can highlight language concepts in the context of a familiar text. Next, he invites the children to illustrate the poem or song. Once a poem or song is ready to be published in the room, Tim and the children share it at gathering time. They read it together several times, often with Tim using a pointer to refer to the words as they are being read. At other times one of the children in the class takes this important responsibility. The children are encouraged to respond to the text by discussing what they like about it. At times, they move to an analysis of the language used in the poem by employing a strategy that Tim calls "What do you notice?"

The strategy began in October when Kareem announced, "Mr. O'Keefe! I've uncovered something!" After reading R. Svec's poem "Could Be Halloween" (Peek 1981), he suggested, "If you cover the first *e* in the word *eyes*, then you have *yes*." Tim capitalized on Kareem's idea and discussed the fact that the entire word changes in both sound and meaning. He invited the others to make observations about the language in the poem. The children made observations about the repetitive story line that concludes each section, connected new words to familiar ones, and experimented with creating new words by changing a letter in a word in the poem. It was Michael who suggested that you can turn the word *back* into *black* by adding an *l*. Megan built upon Michael's idea by noting that words change when you drop letters: "If you cover the *c* and *t* in *cat*, you have the word *a*." Jason noticed that *Halloween* looks a lot like *yellow*. Tim extended this observation by pointing out the low pattern of letters in both words. The children said both words slowly, listening for the similar sounds that these letter combinations make. Derrick continued the discussion about sounds of letters by pointing out the fact that *blinky, blue,* and *black* all begin with *bl* and all sound the same. Several children in the group noticed that the same line is used to conclude each section of the poem.

After reading "A Thanksgiving Poem," Tony responded, "Hey, if you cover up the *t* in *the*, it becomes *he*."

Jason followed by remarking, "That starts like *He-Man*."

In December, the class read P. Watts's "The Snowman and Bunny" (Peek 1981). After several choral reading sessions, Tim asked, "What can you say or what do you notice about this poem?"

Stephen responded, "If you cover the *h* in *his*, it becomes *is*." The group reflected on this insight and said both words aloud, noticing that the *h* did not change the way the *is* part sounds. This observation stemmed from previous language discussions of the situation where a change in just one letter alters the sound of the word significantly, such as Kareem's observation that when you drop the first *e* in *eyes*, the entire word changes its sound and meaning.

Vania's insight redirected the discussion: "In *snowman*, if you cover *snow*, it is just *man*. If you put them both together to make *snowman*, it is like 'plusing.'" Her mathematical insight held true as the group explored other compound words.

Kareem overgeneralized the concept by remarking, "If you cover *ing* in *looking*, you have *look*." Tim acknowledged his observation, but added that *looking* was different than the compound-word examples, in which, following Vania's "plusing" example, both words are complete on their own; he stressed that *ing* was not a whole word.

Vania demonstrated her sensitivity to language again in February when the group reacted to "Ten Little Squirrels." Tim began the discussion by calling their attention to the ordinal numbers in the poem. Vania responded immediately, "That's because of the *th* in those words." She moved to the board and pointed to the *th* in *fourth, fifth,* and *sixth*. Her comment helped the class see the reason and pattern behind this structure in our language.

These are just a few examples that highlight the learning potential inherent in reflecting on the language found in poems and songs. It was the children who suggested that the teacher use this strategy after he introduced new big books. Hence, the same general teaching strategy was flexibly adapted to a new context. Tim found that it was equally effective with big books and, because of the repetitive pattern in many of the predictable books, children were provided opportunities to look for patterns to confirm their predictions.

Reflecting on Language While Writing

Children made connections between certain letters and letters in their names, in favorite words, or in print found in their environment. Often children used letters in each other's names to help them spell new words. When Charles wanted to write about "Tools the Baby Rabbit," a popular class song, he started by saying the word *Tools* slowly. Next, he repeated the initial sound. After a couple of tries, "*t-t-t*," he looked at the message board and read Tony's name. "*T* like in *Tony*," he remarked as he began writing about Tools. This one example highlights a common strategy found in this transition first-grade classroom. Children were encouraged to use each other's names to make connections with letter sounds.

One month earlier, Tony was writing *the* and knew from past reading experiences that it began with a *t*, just like his name. After writing a *t*, he proceeded to write *ony*. He paused, laughed, and commented, "That happens every time I write a *t*." Tim told him that he understood because he was used to associating the letter *t* with his own name. Although there is not a deep phonetic insight in this example, it does emphasize the fact that children make personal connections with letters and sounds. If children are encouraged to use this knowledge and share it with others, the whole class benefits by learning about the letters and sounds in each other's names. When you have a group of eighteen children, with diversely interesting names, the learning potential is rich—so rich that Tim devised another strategy called Name Writing Party in which the children explored letters and sounds in their friends' names.

Vania had demonstrated her awareness of the letters in her friends' names when conducting a survey about butterflies and birds. In the beginning, she took the time to write her friends' complete names. Once she realized that she only had about ten minutes before the beginning of gathering time, she altered her strategy. She decided that she would use the first initial of each respondent's first name. She said she wanted to save time while gathering her data. She soon recognized that her initial idea would only work with certain children. If a child had a name that began with the same letter as other children in the class, then she recorded the initial letter of their first and last names to distinguish between the children. Vania's attempt to clarify various participants in her survey and her decision to use initials to be efficient demonstrated the strategic nature of her thinking.

The children often played with language when working together during free choice time in the morning. One particular morning Stephen, Vania, and Kareem were writing words they knew on the chalkboard. They started with *and*. Just like in the game "What do you notice?" they started experimenting. The next word on their list was *an* because just dropping the *d* made another complete word. They did the same thing with *fall* and *all*. Next, they started generating rhyming words—*hen, pen, cen, fen*—until one member of the group said that *cen* and *fen* were not "real words." (Actually, *fen* is a word, but it is doubtful that the children would have known this word for low land covered in water.) The children then regrouped and tried the strategy again, beginning with the word *bears: bears, fears, pears*, and *sears*. As they proudly reflected on their accomplishment, they realized that although they created real words this time, they did not all sound alike. They noticed that *bears* and *pears* sounded similar and that *fears* was a lot like *Sears*, the store. They continued with *zooms, tooms*, and *fooms*, and concluded that *tooms* and *fooms* were not really words. They tried again with *he, see, we*, and *me*. The children continued to explore their observation about subtle differences in sounds resulting when just one letter changed, and they decided that their latest list showed the consistency in language because they all emphasized the *e* sound in the same way.

Tim was observing this self-directed teaching experience from a distance. He took notes to remember to capitalize on their latest insights about language. As soon as Kareem noticed that Tim was close by, he asked Tim not to erase the board so that they could share their findings with the rest of the class. This experience, like many others described in this chapter, illustrates how children play with written language in ways that are similar to their playing with language from the crib while learning to talk. Capitalizing on such playfulness allows Tim to follow their lead when exploring how language works.

Kareem continued to explore the consistencies and inconsistencies in language as he read. When Tim asked him to write his phone number in his dialogue journal, he looked surprised. *"That's* how you spell *phone?"* he asked. They discussed the spelling, and Kareem noted that he would have spelled it with an *f*. Tim and the rest of the children at the table discussed the fact that sometimes the same letter makes different sounds, depending on the surrounding letters, and often the same sound can be made using different letters, like *f* and *ph*. Although this concept had been raised several times throughout the year, this time the children were so interested that they began looking for both kinds of patterns in their dialogue journals. They used print that they cared about to further their understanding of letter-sound relationships.

Although these examples focus on how children extended their understanding of letters and sounds in language, we do not want to misrepresent the focus on grapheme-phoneme relationships. It was common for the children to address other language issues as well. For instance, when Megan was publishing a book from a story in her journal, she read it aloud to her teacher and a small group of children. She told them that she wanted to know if her story made sense. They responded positively and posed some good questions that would help her strengthen the content of her writing. After spending a couple of writing workshop sessions on revising her book, Megan asked for help again. This time she focused on one particular part of her story. She read, "They rided bicycles." She intuitively knew it needed to be past tense to be consistent with the rest of her text. She asked, "What sounds right, *rided* or *rode?"* The group decided on *rode*.

Tony agreed, " 'They rode bicycles,' definitely."

Thus Megan collaborated with her peers to resolve a problem. Although her first idea, *rided*, was based on the general rule for forming the past tense, Megan did what most authors do when editing their work—she asked whether or not it sounded right. Other examples of children's learning during the writing process are presented in the case studies in chapter 3.

Strategy-Sharing Sessions

Strategy-sharing sessions became one of the most influential teaching strategies in this classroom. During this time, Tim would formally reflect upon the children's learning strategies and share them with the rest of the class. The significance of this strategy went far beyond the specific issues addressed in each session. Because Tim commonly began each session with comments like, "I noticed that Amanda had a good idea . . . ," "Nathan found out . . . ," "Justin made a good observation . . . ," and "Jason devised an effective strategy for . . . ," the children soon became sensitive to the language their teacher was using and began thinking about learning in similar ways. On a daily basis, we found children remarking, "I have a good idea . . . ," "I made an observation . . . ," "I figured out a new way to. . . ." They were reflecting on and valuing their own thinking and then making it explicit so that others might benefit. As a teacher-researcher, Tim always carried a clipboard to document what he considered important insights and ideas. He used his data to direct group conversations during strategy-sharing sessions. Later in the year, many of the children took the lead and described their own strategies to the class.

At the beginning of the year, the children noticed that *Jell-O* looks a lot like *yellow*. Tim shared this observation with the class and held a brief discussion about how the letters *ello* sound the same in both words.

Next, Justin remarked, "Hey, I know another word that begins with the same letter as *Jell-O*."

"Good," responded Tim. "Would you like to write it on the board?"

Justin carefully wrote *Joy* on the board and then said, "That's like a word from church," making the connection between words and their meanings. This comment led to a discussion of how the same word reminds people of different things. *Joy* caused Justin to think about church. His friends offered other possible meanings, including happiness, someone's name, and dishwashing liquid. After this discussion, Tim and the children then returned to words on the board for more strategy sharing.

"Since we have our parakeets in class this week, several of you have been writing about them in the science journal. When Amanda was writing the word *parakeet*, she noticed the double *e*'s in the word. She made an important observation. She said that it was like my name, *O'Keefe*." The children complimented Amanda for the insight and then began generating other words that have two *e*'s together.

Soon after this strategy-sharing session, Tim decided to feature Derrick's thinking. He invited Derrick to the front of the group to explain his work. Derrick proceeded to write *pony* on the board; then he turned to the group and said, "This spells *pony*."

"How do you know?" Tim asked.

"Because I listened to the sounds. I thought that if I added a *p* instead of *t* like in Tony's name, it would be *pony*."

"You have good ideas," remarked Amanda.

Megan added, "Then it rhymes."

Tim confirmed this point and discussed the fact that many

rhyming words are similar in structure, with differences occurring in the beginning sound. Throughout the year, the children had enjoyed creating and finding rhyming words, and so they made immediate connections with Derrick's discovery.

Early in January several new children were enrolled in the transition first-grade classroom. In an effort to make the newcomers feel like a part of the community, Tim suggested that they all make self-portraits to be displayed in the room. He also asked them to write about themselves. He trusted that the children would do the best that they could, and he planned to use his in-process observations to make future teaching decisions. He noticed that Megan and LeeAnn were both slowly saying the words they wanted to write and then identifying salient sounds. Often they would announce the correct name of the letter that made the sound, but were unsure of the letter formation. They would turn to other members of their table and ask how to make a number of letters. LeeAnn's first sentence was *I k to rd a bk,* which meant "I like to ride a bike." Although she selected several important sounds for each word, she needed help writing the letters that she identified by their sounds.

Tim used strategy-sharing sessions to discuss this issue. "Sometimes we know our letters but wonder about their sounds, and other times we can identify the letters by their sounds but aren't sure how to write them. I have noticed that children do both things in our class. I would like to encourage you to work together to help each other identify or write letters. I would like to use LeeAnn's writing as an example today. She did a lovely job of figuring out letters by their sounds, but needed help writing them. Many of you helped her, and I am glad."

Tim noted observations like this in his teacher-researcher notes and used the information to provide timely support for his students. He also integrated this information into his discussion of his own writing.

Games   Tim used games to highlight language concepts. Games were often one of the most popular options during free choice time. Sometimes Tim became an active participant; at other times, the children played independently while he worked with small groups of children on separate projects. As usual, Tim encouraged the children to do much more than simply respond to the games that he provided. He invited them to devise their own games as well.

Megan was one of the first children to accept Tim's invitation to create a game of her own. She created it while she was waiting for her bus after school. Soon after Megan came up with the idea, several of the children joined in. Megan said a word aloud, and the children took turns naming the first letter in the word. "Camel," directed Megan with a grin on her face. Children predicted both *k* and *c*. She pointed to the word *camel* under a picture of a camel on the alphabet card that the children had made for the letter *c* at the beginning of the year. Megan let the child who suggested the letter *c* take the lead for the next round of the game. Tim was pleased with Megan's new game and asked her to teach it to the class the next day.

Tim devoted several minutes to Megan's game during the first morning meeting. He told the class that Megan had created an interesting new game and said that he wanted her to teach the class how to play. She and her bus group demonstrated the game, and then the whole class enthusiastically played it.

After a while, the class came up with an alternative to Megan's original game. They decided to reverse the rules. In the new version, the game leader would think of a letter and then the players had to come up with a word or words that begin with that letter.

A few days later, Megan devised another alternative to her popular letter game. She challenged her friends to come up with the ending letter to words that she posed. This game was somewhat more difficult than the beginning-letter games because many of the words that were generated ended in silent *e*'s or ended in ways that could not be easily identified by sound alone. Tim volunteered to play the game with Megan during gathering time because he wanted to demonstrate effective strategies for solving the new problems. He also capitalized on the opportunity to point out consistencies and inconsistencies in language during his turns.

Child-made board games were also valuable center activities. From the beginning of the year, the children created games and corresponding rules. They often selected themes, such as "The Hurricane Hugo Game," "The Dangerous Animal Game," and "Walk to School." In mid-November, a small group of children began collaborating on a game to represent their ideas about the first Thanksgiving. A snakelike path was drawn across the board with smaller spaces evenly marked. The children wanted the players to portray Native Americans on their way to the first Thanksgiving feast. Along the way they would encounter obstacles, such as trees in the path and dangerous animals. When players landed on spaces too close to these obstacles, they had to move back a designated number of spaces or lose a turn. Likewise, there were shortcuts the Native Americans could take if they landed on certain spaces. In addition to being thoughtfully planned, the board was colorfully decorated with trees, ponds, and a delicious-looking feast at the end of the path.

When devising the playing rules for the Thanksgiving game, it was Vania who suggested a spinner with alphabet letters (see Figure 36). "Let's do the ABCs. When the kids land on the letter, they say the ABCs." Vania demonstrated her idea by moving her piece along the gameboard while singing the alphabet. Each space represented one letter, so if the spinner landed on the letter *f*, the player would move six spaces. As the children played the game, they rehearsed the sequence of the alphabet and quickly came to realize the relationship between letters in order. Insights gained through playing this game lent themselves to early alphabetizing— the letter *b* allowed them to move two spaces, while the letter *f* advanced them six spaces.

Name-Writing Party

Following the children's lead, Tim devised a Name-Writing Party in early September. He had noticed during journal writing that several children were copying names from the alphabetized roster in the front of the room. He was also aware that the children were making observations about similarities and differences in names: "*Jessica, Justin,* and *Jason* all begin with the letter *j*." To foster this interest, one journal-writing period was devoted solely to name writing. The children and teachers donned their name tags, picked up a pen or pencil and their journals, and began recording each other's names. Because the children were wearing their name tags, they began to associate faces with the print that represented their peers' names. The children used their journals to report their observations at gathering time.

"The *ee* in your name, Mr. O'Keefe, is just like *Kareem*," Justin noticed. The class chimed in. Some children focused on the beginning letters of names. Others attended to the way names ended. As they conversed, Tim confirmed their ideas and clarified their observations. Because the children were naturally interested in their friends' names, this strategy provided a rich opportunity to explore letter-sound combinations in familiar print.

Although the formal name-writing party took place early in the year, the children continued to pursue this valuable strategy throughout the year during free choice time. As the year progressed, their observations became more sophisticated. They also transferred the focus of this experience to other contexts. In early February, Justin was carefully examining Tim's class roster on his clipboard. A page of Tim's field notes partially covered the list. Looking at the first letters of the children's last names, Justin remarked, "I see three last names that begin with *J*. And if I move

Figure 36
Spinner for the Thanksgiving game.

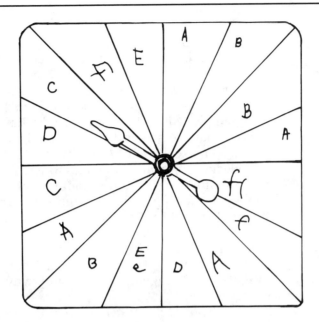

the paper over I see *Je, Je, Jo*. If I move the paper over again I see *Jen, Jen, Joh*. Look at how they are almost the same."

Tim asked him to continue exploring this pattern. "Move the paper a little further and see what you find out."

"I see *Jenk, Jenn, John* now." As Justin added additional letters, he developed better clues that would help him distinguish the last names. Tim pointed out how they needed to look at the fourth letter to determine whether or not they were reading *Jenkins* or *Jennings*.

Tim asked, "Do you see any other cases like this one, similar names?"

Justin moved to the *R*s. He covered all but the first letter and declared, "Three *R* names." He moved the paper slightly and then revised his observation, "*Re, Re, Re*! They are all the same so far." He continued, "*Red, Ree, Reg*. That's as far as you can go for them to be the same."

Tim immediately saw the learning potential in this experience and so invited Justin to share his observations with the class. They had a rich, informative discussion about common letter patterns in names and then began to explore familiar words in the room. They played the game using Justin's original plan. Tim wrote several words on the board that began with the same letter. He covered all of the print except the beginning letter and asked the children to predict the words he had written. He moved the paper over one letter and asked them to confirm or revise their original thoughts, continuing until the children guessed the words.

Additional Strategies   In addition to the strategies listed above, children learn about letter-sound relationships during authentic reading experiences. However, as demonstrated in chapter 2, children are encouraged to use multiple cue systems simultaneously to construct meaning. They often make predictions based on using syntactic and semantic cues. For example, when Tony was asked what he did when he came to a word that he did not know, he replied, "All I do is look at the words to make sense of the other words." The children used knowledge of graphophonemics to test these predictions in combination with syntactic and semantic cues. Vania pointed out her strategy in dealing with the word *cap:* "This word was in my book. At first I thought it was *cat,* but then I put the *p* at the end and I just read it." The word *cat* did not make sense in her story, so she made use of semantic and syntactic cues to read *cap.* The previous chapters provide other examples that demonstrate the kinds of insights about language that are interwoven throughout reading experiences.

Chapter 2 illustrates the rich learning opportunities that editing for publication provides children. It was inevitable that Tim would find genuine opportunities to help children refine their understanding about graphophonemic knowledge when they were preparing a piece for publication. They understood the value of invented spelling and became very comfortable using it when composing. As they constructed their own spellings for new words, they often used and generated knowledge about letter-sound relationships. They also understood that it was important to edit drafts if they were publishing for a broad audience. When helping children edit their pieces, Tim and Sandra consistently acknowledged the similarity of the children's invented spellings to the standard versions: "Look how close you were. You just need to add an *e* at the end of the word. I know you don't hear that sound when you say the word slowly. Let's look for any other words that might have a silent *e* in your story." Chapters 2 and 3 feature editing experiences and clearly show how such knowledge is embedded within authentic literacy events. Language conventions are put into their proper perspective. They are valued because they help us communicate effectively as readers and writers. And as children edit their work, they develop important understandings about language.

Why Were These Strategies So Effective?

When we review all of the teaching strategies presented above, it is clear that they are very diverse. Some focus on the whole class, while others work most successfully with individual children. Some are formal, planned experiences; others happen incidentally. At times, the strategy emerges from the children, while at other times, Tim generates the idea based on careful "kidwatching." The uniqueness of each teaching strategy does not imply an "eclectic" perspective or even inconsistent planning. Instead, if we look beyond the surface structure of each opportunity, we uncover a great deal of commonality. These strategies are united by the following assumptions about the learning process:

1. Children learn best when the experiences are open-ended and choices are provided.
2. Children learn best when they work together and are encouraged to learn from each other.
3. Children learn best when they connect new insights to familiar or functional print.
4. Children learn best through demonstration, engagement, and reflection.
5. Children learn best when they are encouraged to pose their own questions and test their hypotheses.
6. Children learn best when they are provided opportunities to celebrate their insights and growth.
7. Children learn best when teachers function as participants, guides, and learners in their classrooms.

This list does not encompass all of the characteristics of Tim's curriculum. It does, however, show the very basic assumptions that underpin his teaching. Tim attempts to teach in ways that are consistent with the learning process. His teaching strategies reflect what is currently known about learners and learning. Through his own classroom research, he contributes to the body of literature that we currently have about language, teaching, and learning.

Afterword

We embarked upon this project because of the attention that has been drawn to the role of phonics in whole language classrooms. Many parents, teachers, and administrators frequently ask us about phonics instruction. Their questions, while sincere, often reflect misconceptions about whole language. The comments of one language arts coordinator capture this misunderstanding: "We would support whole language, but we are afraid our students would not learn anything about phonics." In the past, our responses to such charges have been grounded in our understanding of the process and in our observations of children's learning. We "knew" children were learning about letter-sound relationships as they were reading and writing. However, we had not systematically explored this issue. When we decided to take a closer look at the role of the graphophonemic cue system in Tim's curriculum and at the language growth of several children in his classroom, we found ourselves understanding more about the powerful role that all the cue systems, including grapheme-phoneme relationships, play in written language learning.

The Paradox   It may seem paradoxical to attempt to write about graphophonemic instruction from a "whole" language perspective because, in whole language classrooms, children use all cue systems simultaneously to construct meaning. Therefore, to focus on one feature, in this case letter-sound relationships, seems to contradict the very premise upon which the whole language model is built. However, we felt that we better understood whole language as a result of having taken a close look at the role of this cue system within the whole language classroom. We hope the reader will reach a similar conclusion.

In conducting our research, we adopted a photography metaphor. When we stood back and examined language as a whole, like a photographer viewing a landscape through a wide-angle lens, we learned certain things about the process of language learning. As we changed to a zoom lens and focused on the graphophonemic cue system, we were able to take a different perspective and thus learn different things. Clearly, graphophonemics is only valuable when used in conjunction with syntax and semantics to support the construction of meaning. In the past (and, unfortunately, in the present in some classrooms at some times), phonics instruction has been mistakenly taught as an end in itself, with little or no connection to meaning. Alternatively, in some classrooms at some times, teachers, particularly whole language teachers, have been accused of teaching syntax and semantics, but not teaching phonics. We hope that this text will illustrate that children do develop an understanding of letter-sound relationships while using and learning language in a whole language classroom.

This book is not meant to be an instructional document that tells teachers how to "teach" sound-symbol relationships. Instead, it shows how Tim taught his children, and encouraged them to teach each other, by responding to their questions and interests. Tim believes it is his right and responsibility to teach responsively. Following his lead, we believe it would be a violation of our model to ignore genuine questions from our colleagues concerning phonics and whole language. This text thus represents not an end, but perhaps a helpful beginning. We hope it has answered some questions and sparked new ones. It has done so for us.

References

Adams, M. J. 1990. *Beginning to Read: Thinking and Learning about Print.* Cambridge, Mass.: MIT Press.

Church, S., and J. Newman. 1985. "Danny: A Case History of an Instructionally Induced Reading Problem." In *Whole Language: Theory in Use,* edited by J. Newman. Portsmouth, N.H.: Heinemann.

DeFord, D. 1981. "Literacy: Reading, Writing and Other Essentials." *Language Arts* 58(6): 652–58.

DeLawler, J. 1985. "The Relationship of Beginning Reading Instruction and Miscue Patterns." In *Help for the Reading Teacher: New Directions in Research,* edited by W. Page. Urbana, Ill.: National Council of Teachers of English.

Durr, W. K., and R. L. Hillerich. 1983. *Getting Ready to Read.* Boston: Houghton-Mifflin.

Freppon, P., and K. Dahl. 1991. "Learning about Phonics in a Whole Language Classroom." *Language Arts* 68(3): 190–97.

Goodman, K. S. 1967. "Reading: A Psycholinguistic Guessing Game." *Journal of the Reading Specialist* 4:126–35.

Goodman, Y. 1985. "Kidwatching: Observing Children in the Classroom." In *Observing the Language Learner,* edited by A. Jaggar and M. Trika Smith-Burke. Newark, Del.: International Reading Association.

Halliday, M.A.K. 1982. "Three Aspects of Children's Language Development: Learning Language, Learning through Language, Learning about Language." In *Oral and Written Language Development Research: Impact on the Schools,* edited by Y. Goodman, M. H. Haussler, and D. Strickland, 7–19. Urbana, Ill.: National Council of Teachers of English.

Harste, J. C., and C. L. Burke. 1977. "A New Hypothesis for Reading Teacher Research: Both *Teaching* and *Learning* of Reading Are Theoretically Based." In *Reading: Theory, Research, and Practice, Twenty-Sixth Yearbook of the National Reading Conference,* edited by P. D. Pearson and J. Hansen. Clemson, S.C.: National Reading Conference. ED 227 440.

Mills, H., and J. A. Clyde. 1990. *Portraits of Whole Language Classrooms: Learning for All Ages.* Portsmouth, N.H.: Heinemann.

———. 1991. "Children's Success as Readers and Writers: It's the Teacher's Reliefs That Make the Difference." *Young Children* 46:54–59.

Peek, P. P., comp. 1981. *Performable Poems.* Middletown, Conn.: Weekly Reader.

Smith, F. 1978. *Understanding Reading.* New York: Holt, Rinehart and Winston.

Stahl, S. J., J. Osborn, and F. Lehr. 1990. *Beginning to Read: Thinking and Learning about Print: A Summary.* Champaign, Ill.: Center for the

Study of Reading, University of Illinois at Urbana-Champaign. Report available from the Center for the Study of Reading.

Stice, C., and N. Bertrand. 1989. "The Texts and Textures of Literacy Learning in Whole Language versus Traditional Skills Classrooms." In *Thirty-Eighth Yearbook of the National Reading Conference,* edited by S. McCormick and J. Zutell. Rochester, N.Y.: National Reading Conference.

Whiten, D., H. Mills, and T. O'Keefe. 1990. *Living and Learning Mathematics: Stories and Strategies for Supporting Mathematical Literacy.* Portsmouth, N.H.: Heinemann.

Willert, M., and C. Kamii. 1985. "Reading in Kindergarten: Direct versus Indirect Teaching." *Young Children* 40:3–9.

Authors

Heidi Mills is an assistant professor of elementary education at the University of South Carolina. She is currently involved in the fourth year of a collaborative research project with teacher Timothy O'Keefe and university colleague David Whitin. Together they are exploring how children learn language and mathematics and ways to develop curricular experiences that are consistent with the learning process. Their book *Living and Learning Mathematics: Stories and Strategies for Supporting Mathematical Literacy* reflects their initial inquiry. Mills's interest in supporting whole language teachers resulted in *Portraits of Whole Language Classrooms: Learning for All Ages*, which she coedited with Jean Anne Clyde.

Timothy O'Keefe has been teaching early childhood and elementary education for thirteen years. He has taught all grade levels from preschool through sixth grade, including compensatory and transition classrooms. As a classroom researcher and collaborator with university colleagues Heidi Mills and David Whitin, O'Keefe and his classroom have been the focus of several chapters, books, and videotape series. His transition first-grade classroom is featured in this book as well as in *Living and Learning Mathematics: Stories and Strategies for Supporting Mathematical Literacy* and *Visions of Literacy*, a videotape series.

Diane Stephens has taught a variety of learners in a variety of settings over the last twenty years, including individuals with learning difficulties. After receiving her Ph.D. from Indiana University, she developed an interdisciplinary clinic at the University of North Carolina–Wilmington. She and teachers from that area coauthored a book, *What Matters? A Primer for Teaching Reading*, based on their experiences in the clinic. Currently at the Center for the Study of Reading, University of Illinois at Urbana-Champaign, Stephens conducts research in her own and other classrooms. She also teaches undergraduate and graduate literacy courses for the College of Education.